Thoughts Along The Way

Books by Ben Mukkala:

"Thoughts Along the Way - Secrets of a Happy Life" Selected Columns

"Life is Not a Destination"

Audio Version, "Life is Not a Destination"

"Touring Guide, Big Bay & Huron Mountains"

"Come On Along, Tales and Trails of the North Woods"

"Copper, Timber, Iron and Heart, Stories from Michigan's Upper Peninsula"

Thoughts Along the Way

by

Ben Mukkala

Still Waters Publishing
Marquette, Michigan
© 2007

Thoughts Along the Way

All photography in this book is the work of the author
unless indicated otherwise.

Published by
Still Waters Publishing, 2007

Printing Coordinated by
Globe Printing, Ishpeming, Michigan
www.globeprinting.net

Limited First Edition • 2,000 copies • November 2007

ISBN   978-0-9709971-6-6

Dedication

"... The purpose of life is to *matter* – to count, to stand for something, to have it make some difference that we have lived at all."

Leo C. Rosten

This book is respectfully dedicated to

You,

The Reader

If these pages inform you, if you enjoy them, if they give a little insight, warm your heart, if they lighten your burdens even just for a day, then I have "made some difference," I have "mattered."

Acknowledgements

This page is to acknowledge the help received from others. It's in recognition of those I couldn't have done without - and a plea for forgiveness to those I have disappointed. I don't guess it interests you who read the book but it fulfills an obligation and confesses personal shortcomings.

In appreciation I should include all those who taught me about life and living, the standards and ethics by which I believe a "good" person should abide. A fella's mother and father immediately come to mind - and the memory of a Grandfather who coughed his life away after working for years in the copper mines. Then too there were a couple of wars along the way. There's nothing like the impersonal terror of war-up-close to tear the tinsel from the fundamentals of life.

For the immediate task I must thank my wife, Dorothy, for her never failing encouragement, my friend and fellow author Jerry Harju for his editing and "tearing me up" over style, Mrs. Stacey Willey who never hesitated to tell me if I was about to screw something up and those kind folks who read and commented on my work in the past – Thank You. Responsibility for mistakes of course is mine.

Last but not least I wish to thank you folks who choose to read these pages. Without you there would be no need for any of it.

Enjoy! I hope I don't disappoint you.

Table of Contents

Forward

A fundamental belief of so many of the world's philosophers comes down to this: Each of us wishes to be treated kindly, with empathy, fairly and honestly. Doesn't it follow that we should treat others kindly, with empathy, fairly and honestly?

"Do not do to others that which would anger you if others did it to you." Socrates: (Greece; 5th century B.C.)

The clearest guidance you can give your children, grandchildren or anybody else is not by what you say but by the things you do and how you do them. Your examples speak louder than your words.

When someone you love is sick or injured, especially if it's a child, how often do you wish you could hurt for them, could bear their pain? And what a warm feeling of satisfaction and enjoyment we get when the things we do are able help others. Never mind what others say or do, we're talking about you.

"Every religion emphasizes human improvement, love, respect for others, sharing other people's suffering. On these lines every religion had more or less the same viewpoint and the same goal." The Dalai Lama

I hope, in the stories that follow, you find ways this applies to you and me.

Ben Mukkala

The first indication that you're learning anything comes when you realize how much you still don't know.

Thoughts Along The Way

The Natural Elusion

I haven't been up here for quite a while, not since the snow's been gone anyway. The leaves are out. Strawberry blossoms, Thimbleberry blossoms, apple blossoms are all bursting forth. Wintergreen berries peak shyly from beneath their waxen green leaves. Ferns are spreading their green canopy near the ground. Some of the ferns haven't spread out yet; they're still in the little balled-up-fist stage. A person can pluck that little fist off and eat it. It tastes, well, I guess I'd have to say it tastes a little like asparagus. City folks wouldn't do that of course. If it didn't come from a store shelf it isn't something you should put in your mouth. Just after my son, Benny, got married I tried to introduce his new bride to this delicacy of our world. She was from down in the Detroit area.

She was very polite, took the offered morsel from me but I noticed she surreptitiously threw it away when she didn't think I was looking. No matter. It's Benny she's married to, not me. She's probably glad about that too, glad that he's not like his crusty old father, an escapee from some northern swamp. There were the tracks of a doe and her fawn along the road as I came in. I stopped to examine them more closely.

The temperature is just sixty something degrees up here in the woods. A light breeze wafts through the trees, just enough to set the leaves moving. It's not summer yet but it's gettin' close.

Lord, the memories that are here. I remember as a young kid hunting these woods with my father and the bunch of guys who used to gather here every deer season. They were good days, good memories. I brought my son up here too but he was raised more in the cities where I was stationed while in the Air Force. He's not really attuned to the outdoors. Shucks, I've brought my grandsons up here. They were a bit concerned one afternoon that a bear was about to get them but it was only their grandpa hidden in the brush rustling the bushes and growling. I think they'll remember that experience though. Later we all roasted hot dogs over an open fire.

Darn! I just plucked a wood tick off of the back of my neck. Well, it's that time of year. I guess wood ticks have their place in the great scheme of things too.

The sun's a little brighter now. There are broken

clouds but they're clearing up. It feels warmer in the sunshine.

There's an old jar of mints on the kitchen shelf. They've got to have been there since, lessee – I would guess those candies are almost as old as some of you kids who are graduating high school this spring. They've settled into a thick soupy mess in the bottom of their jar. I'll scrape the mixture out onto the ground and leave it for the ants and other critters. I'll take the jar, a rather pretty old jar, home and clean it up.

You know, in the old days, the thirties and forties, it was customary to leave a vacant cabin with firewood and a few canned goods on the shelf. The thinking back then was that if someone were lost or had had an accident back in the bush, especially in winter, there'd be a refuge for them. There was a lock on the door but it was mostly for show and to keep the riff-raff out. It would have been easily broken by anyone serious about getting in. This place, shucks the whole area was a lot more remote back then. The practice of stocking a cabin could mean the difference between someone surviving or not. It seems, back when life was a lot tougher, when everyone was scratching hard folks were more inclined to look out for one another. Small towns still seem to retain some of that. The inclination in the bigger cities tends toward "dog eat dog and the first bite counts the most."

But those aren't the memories I'm sitting with at the moment. The "Natural Elusion" I named the place. It was nature all around and it was a good place to "elude" the cares of the rest of the world. As an aside, cell phones don't work up here either just in case you're interested.

A fella approached me about buying the place a while ago. None of my kids seems interested in my old shack in the woods. Well, I'm interested in it yet. I don't get here very often but I never fail to enjoy the tranquility and the memories when I do. That remains true even when there are patch-up fix-up things to do. I think I'll just hang onto the place and let the kids decide what to do what to do when it's time to share "my estate."

Good Morning

It's morning, early morning. The sun is just peeking above the horizon lighting up a clear blue sky. It's not an indigo blue as it is with the stars still out but a sort of powder blue heralding a beautiful new day. The "big lake," Lake Superior, is a sheet of glass, not a ripple nor even a "cat's paw" marring the surface. The powder blue sky is reflected perfectly with barely a line denoting the horizon. It looks like it's going to be a beautiful day.

Wispy puffs of fog, morning mist, gently drift across the still waters of the bayou. A couple of ducks, the fighter pilots of the aviary world rise from the mist and rocket across the scene going to wherever it is that ducks go in the early morning. A lone seagull drifts by, its head scanning left and right, wings moving methodically and mechanically in its eternal quest for something to eat – and it'll eat darn near anything.

The house is quiet and still. Dorothy hasn't gotten up yet. There hasn't even been a car passing out on the road either. Well, it's Saturday morning and many people don't have to go to work today. I look down at our bayou bridge. The bridge runs about 800 feet or so across both open water and marsh to the beach. I'm kind of proud of that bridge. It started with a pencil and a sheet of paper and the desire to get to the beach without having to walk across the neighbor's property. So there it is. The ice and snow of winter can be rough on the framework. Every spring I have to reset a drum or two, pump a little air into them. But it's worth it.

I would guess that most of us who live in Upper Michigan have a feeling for the "big lake." That's especially true for those of us who live along the shore or who have spent a bit of our lives working out on that wide expanse of water. If you've ever watched the sunrise while out there – well – I guess you've got to experience it. A person learns respect! If you don't learn respect that lake'll getcha. As I stand looking across the bayou it's quiet as only early morning can be. The emerging world is beautiful.

Two of our young grandsons stopped by yesterday just before supper. They were with their momma on their way home to Sundell. Mary knows how fond Dorothy and I are of Levi and Hudson and she stops by frequently. The boys gave us a hug, checked out the bayou, searched for and found the little chocolate candies grandma and I always hide for them. Then, as grandma and momma talked, the boys sprawled in front of the television watching whatever the current kid's show was. As I look out across the bayou remembering their visit yesterday I remember too that I was about their age when I first came to this bayou. The parents of a playmate, Jimmy Smeberg, owned a camp on the point. They used to bring Jimmy and me out with them and we'd play on the bayou and the beach. That was a good while ago. There have been many sunrises over this bayou since then. How long and how twisted was my path through life since those bygone days. Watching my grandsons I wonder what the world holds in store for them. I wonder if they, when they're my age, will look across this bayou and think these thoughts.

They're absorbed in their television program. I can't help but wish there were some way I could protect them, shield them from some of the blunders, the missteps their grandpa has made. But, of course, you can't do that. We've each got to find our own way. Love 'em, tell 'em, teach them as much as you can but they've got to find their own way in life.

Watching the bayou coming alive this morning I know that each of those creatures has adapted to the world into which it was born. Life and death are their close companions and a part of their everyday existence. I doubt that they dwell on such thoughts. I doubt they are even aware that that's the way it is. It's that way with us too. I know this - and so do you - but we try to ignore it don't we?

The aroma of fresh brewed coffee drifts quietly into my reverie. A seagull arcs down and perches on the porch railing. It's anticipating my regular scattering of bread and corn each morning. The bayou is brighter now as the sun clears the horizon. I automatically reach for a cup from the cupboard and fill it with fresh coffee.

Then I pour orange juice into my coffee. *!#. Oh, shut up! I know what you're thinking. Down the drain with it! Pour another cup and start over, this time with a little cream. A new day has begun.

CR

Independence

Once a week a bunch of us "Old Timers" get together down at the Marquette's Senior Center for coffee. Once a month we'll splurge and go out for breakfast at some local restaurant. We collect a buck each for the coffee meetings and, when there's enough in the kitty, we take our ladies out for lunch at a local restaurant somewhere. It's more than just coffee or breakfast or lunch with the ladies though. It keeps us all in touch with one another, keeps us up on local news, and provides for an exchange of ideas and even a joke or two at times. We're all still functional.

There's another little ceremony we do at our meetings: we have an American Flag in the room and some time during our "bull" session one of the guys'll stand up and initiate it. We then all stand and recite the Pledge of Allegiance ". . . to the flag of the United States of America and to . . ." This is followed by a group singing of one stanza of the national anthem. One of the guys will then read a short self-composed prayer aloud. Making allowance for the singing – and the Lord knows an allowance is required – it's an inspiring inset. You might suggest that these actions are only symbolic things. You'd be right! That symbolism was why they were created.

These simple acts demonstrate our unity (as opposed to anarchy) and serve as a reminder, to quote the phrase, that "freedom is not free." The Pledge of Allegiance is not just something the kids are told do in school each morning. There's meaning and dedication in those words. I hope the kids are still reciting the Pledge of Allegiance in school each morning. I tried to check on that by telephone with local area schools. Maybe it's because of summer vacations but my calls were mostly answered by, "Hello, you have reached ..." I was talking to a machine. "Press button . . ." At the Gwinn School a real live person, someone with a pulse answered the phone. They didn't have an immediate answer to my question but they did call back later. They assured me the pledge was done each day. I believe the observation of these ceremonies, knowledge of why it is recited is an important factor in assuring the survival of our nation and our way of life.

When I stand with the fellas at the Old Timers coffee and recite that pledge I feel camaraderie, a unity, you could even call it brotherhood. Some of the old timers are former soldiers, sailors, marines, guys who served time in the military service. Some have been shot at – and shot back - and people were dying on both sides. These were significant periods in their lives and in the life of the country but that's not what I'm talking about just now. I'm talking about the unity thing. We may each vigorously disagree with one another but these simple acts of unity are recognition that we're all going in the same direction.

Now let's see if I can toe-dance around this religion thing a little. These United States were founded by people of deep religious conviction. Previous experience led these founders to acknowledge and accept that, in spite of their own beliefs, other citizens should not be required to accept and adhere to that belief. They needn't profess any religion at all for that matter. The founding principles of the constitution, the country and the government however had been and still are shaped by a philosophy as put forth in Judeo Christian teachings. No one has to involve any god to be able to accept these ideas: equality before the law, treat other people the way you wish to be treated, recognize the need for a government where majority rules but the minority is protected. Accept the fact that your right to swing your fist stops just short of the other fella's nose. As we use to say in the military, "As long as it doesn't hurt me or the old soldier's home it's OK".

There are times when "radical activists," atheists, whatever proclaim loud and long that some action or the lack thereof will end the world as we know it. Hear them out. This is the great melting pot and sometimes they say something of significance. It was "radicals" with new ideas that shaped this nation. Severe and limited restrictions on what people were allowed to think created a period in history now referred to as "the dark ages." Hear them out. New ideas created our way of life, the envy of most of the world, but the price of our freedoms is eternal vigilance. Pay attention. Get off your butt and at least vote even if you aren't politically active otherwise.

Well, that's the way I believe it should be. And I think that's where many of the "Old Timers" stand too. I hope some of the rest of you think that way because when I get to be the king . . . .

CR

It Doesn't Get Any Better

A person never stands so tall
As when they stoop to help a child.

I got up this morning about a quarter to seven. The sun was up, the sky was clear; a couple of geese were preening themselves on a log in the bayou. It looked like the beginning of a beautiful day. It was a little chilly at 40 degrees but a beautiful day none the less.

I've got an exercise routine I go through every morning - and I hate it. I carry it out religiously though. It's the price I pay to remain "functional" as the weight of the years bears down on me. I usually try to record a TV program the night before to distract me during the exercise but, at least for me, a "good" TV program is pretty scarce. Enough of that! This is about a good day. First let me tell you about it and then we'll talk.

Thursday mornings about 9:30 AM I go by the

Chocolay Children's Center. They allow me to "read" to the children for a short time. The kids are, say, six and under so their attention span is short. When I walked in the door they were gathered in a circle on the floor with one of the ladies conducting – whatever it was. She lost control immediately. The kids jumped up and rushed over to give "poppa Ben" a big hug, all of them (including my two grandsons). I love it! I have to admit to a prejudice here. I have always believed that any one from whom children or dogs shy away, well, you had better look at that person pretty carefully before trusting them about anything.

I always try to bring the kids something that'll get their interest, something related to the book or story I'm going to tell. After the greeting, we all sit down on the floor, all of us. They all want to sit in my lap and I do the best I can to accommodate them. Then we'll sort of fight over the book and which page we'll talk about. There's not much reading what with page-turning and kids crawling all over me and talking and everything at once. I talk louder than they do so I kind of hold the floor. The folks who run the center stay in the room with us and have several times offered me a chair. This would place me above and away from the children. Not on your life! We all pile up on the floor together. Someone wants to look at my hearing aid. A couple more want to turn the pages – some want to go forward and maybe a couple others want to go back. Somebody wants to tell me something but, without my hearing aid, I have trouble understanding them. With everyone talking at once I have trouble understanding them anyway. I don't know if they get anything from my stories but we all seem to have a good time. I especially try to reach out to the shy ones so we can include everybody. Sometimes it works and sometimes, well, that's the way it goes. Finally, after fifteen or twenty minutes, I sort of extricate myself. Everyone gets and gives a final hug, especially for the shy ones, and I'm on my way until next week.

My next stop is for coffee and a late, light breakfast. A couple of folks are looking over the books that are for sale at the cafe. I boldly ask if there's anything I can tell them about "those books." They ask if I know anything about them. I tell them that I'm the guy who wrote them. We talk briefly and discover that we have mutual friends and a shared past. They buy a book and ask me to autograph it. I'm flattered. I'm also shameless! How sweet it is!

During this interlude another couple with their young son comes in. The youngster is a little shy and it takes some negotiating to decide what he wants to drink. I finish my coffee, pay for my breakfast and, as I am leaving, pause beside the young man. I look at him intently. He returns my gaze although a little uncertainly. Then I squat down – it's important in communicating with children that you put yourself on their level – and I say, "I see what your problem is." This confuses the lad. He didn't know he had a problem. The parents are a little uncertain about me but choose to watch what develops. I ask him, "What's that in your ear?" There's more confusion and uncertainty as he reaches up and feels his ear. I reach out – and take a quarter from the boy's ear. "You shouldn't put money in your ear. Here. Put that in your pocket." What's he going to do? Uncertain, he turns to his momma. Both parents are into it now and are smiling. I get up and head for the door with a sort of finger-waving goodbye as I go. The boy stares at the quarter in his hand. His momma says, "Thank you." Thank me? I should be thanking you! Where else can you buy so much happiness for a quarter?

To do these things you've got to put yourself out – expose your ego. The child, children, or the parents may think you're some kind of nut and turn away, shut you down, freeze you out so to speak. If your self-image is fragile, if deep down inside your confidence, your self-esteem is at all weak, you yourself may feel damaged, slighted, put down by the rejection. Don't be! When it works, the payoff is well worth the risk. If you stop to think about it, the reason more of us aren't more successful at anything and everything in life is that we're afraid to fail. Remember, he - or she - who risks nothing, gains nothing. Suck it up and give 'er a shot but always remember, don't talk AT the child, talk TO them. There's a difference.

Well, that's how my morning started. And you know what? I don't care what happens this afternoon. A day that starts like this one has gotta be a good day.

CR

It's All Right Here!

It's a beautiful day! It's about two o'clock in the afternoon. There are scattered clouds drifting across a soft blue sky. The sun is bright and friendly shining on everything and everybody. A soft breeze wafts in from the southwest. The temperature is about seventy degrees. It doesn't get any better than this. Dorothy and I live along Lake Superior and have easy access to the beach – which is where I am going at the moment.

To get to the beach we've got to cross a bayou that's about half marsh and half open water, a distance of about 800 feet. We used to walk around the edge of the bayou but that entailed crossing a couple of neighbor's properties. As more and more people moved in we no longer knew all the neighbors as well as we once did. This led to our visiting the beach less and less and finally almost never.

We decided that had to change. We consulted with the Environmental Protection Agency and with local Zoning officials. We solicited the advice and comments of a few friends and finally took a critical look at our bank account. I rolled up my sleeves and lit into the task. The gods of marshes and swamps didn't always look favorably on fools such as I. There were several days I spent working in muck up to my knees. I fell into pot holes – one so deep that the only thing the remained on the surface was my hat. It wasn't an easy job what with the rules laid down by the Environmental Protection Agency and all but we did it! We now cross the open water on a bridge floating on empty drums. We traverse the marsh on a slightly elevated walkway resting on logs.

As I walk along I can't help but secretly feel kind of proud of my accomplishment. I think it's a pretty - whup – wait a minute. What's that just ahead of me? It looks like – it IS. A raccoon has left his calling card right in the middle of my walk. I wonder if that raccoon was casual and careless or if he's trying to tell me something. With a flick of the toe of my shoe I eliminate his comment from my walkway and move on.

The next project to come to mind was to build a small "beach-house." It would be a place for changing clothes or just sitting and reading or – whatever - but it would be protected from the cool winds – and snow - of fall and winter. Once again the project entails a trip to consult the powers that be, the Zoning Administrator, to check on the rules. "Well, you can't build within 50 feet of high water and the beach and etc. etc." Things were looking pretty bleak. "But, if the building is less than 100 square feet none of these rules will apply." My little beach house is 8' x 12' (I'll let you do the math). It's all glassed in so a person doesn't ever miss any of the view.

Of course our little beach house has picked up a whole lot of this and that, little conveniences stored "for the beach." So it goes. I've discovered the secret is not to get too involved with details. Just enjoy things as they are – don't make waves. (Oooh, that remark fit in there well, didn't it?)

As I arrive the breeze is cool and gentle. The waves roll onto the beach with a "whish." They seem to be calling in hushed tones, inviting me to come for a swim. The rustling leaves of the maple trees sigh contentedly in the passing breeze. The beach grass waves casually, bending with the wind. Suddenly all is still – but only for a moment. The wind picks up again.

Spackles of sunshine flash through the windows and dance across the floor. Clouds drift by gradually changing shape as they pass then fading away to disappear as they move out over the lake. On the lake the waves smile at me showing their teeth occasionally as they make their way toward the shore.

The deep blue of the lake fades to an emerald green as it approaches shallow water. The water is even brighter green where it crosses a sand bar. The sand bars themselves are transient things moving ever so slowly as the waves and currents dictate. Nearer the shoreline the emerald color fades to a soft, sandy brown. Having owned a couple boats and sailed around out there I almost feel the lake is lonesome, calling me to come back. We've had some good times, that lake and I – and a couple of real "nail biters" too. That's the sort of thing that provides spice to life!

Maybe what I see and hear in all this has something to do with being born here? Or maybe it's just age and learning to slow life down, to take the time to realize what beauty and wonders are all around us wherever we are. It's probably a bit of both. I've been fortunate in my life. I've had many exciting experiences. I've been able to travel to many places, in both the Northern and Southern Hemispheres and several points along the way. I watch as the sun goes down. After all is said and done right here is where I want to be. How about you?

CR

Lest We Forget

It's a bit early to be talking about Fourth of July but bear with me. This has to do with planning ahead. Many of you may know – or may not know - that it was the dedicated efforts of the men and women of Marquette's Richard M. Jopling Post # 44 of the American Legion that created the Marquette Area Veteran's Memorial. It stands quietly and unobtrusively in Harlow Park in Marquette. The original dedication took place on November 11, 2002, the day we celebrate as "Veteran's Day." We used to call it "Armistice Day" commemorating the end of World War I, the "War to end all Wars."

Well, it was a good thought but unfortunately it wasn't – wasn't the "War that ended all Wars," that is. Wars kept happening. More and more men and women were called to fill the ranks of our military. And whenever they were called they came. This is what the Harlow Park Memorial is all about.

When the idea of a Marquette Area Veteran's Memorial was first conceived it was decided it would not be a "War" memorial. It would be a memorial to all, to all the men and women who answered or are now answering the country's call - in peace or in war. It includes all service members in any branch of service, anyone at all from the Marquette area. The "Marquette Area." That swings a pretty wide loop around the central Upper Peninsula. Because of its nature this memorial is not a static display but a continuing, growing and on-going thing.

Since its original dedication a memorial service has been held there each Fourth of July. At each memorial service the names of unlisted Veterans, those who have been nominated over the previous year are added to the rolls.

If you might wish to explore the memorial, review the names already thereon, there is a convenient way. The roll is catalogued with the names of over 1600 veterans already memorialized. There is a map of the memorial walkway providing the location of each individual veteran's marker. To explore the memorial further, to see if someone you know may be there, go to this web site: www.superiorfishing.net.

Today's headlines seem to focus on a Presidential trip abroad, the Vice President trying to avoid the news, a Senator objecting to some bill or a Representative who may or may not have given special consideration to a lobbyist. Meanwhile, each passing day, some soldier may have been killed in Iraq, another may have been injured in Afghanistan. Worldwide – including at home here in the United States - many more servicemen and women are resolutely going about the business of protecting the nation, standing guard – standing guard for you and me.

But that's old news. That's no longer sensational, front-page news. But where would we be without them? They've quietly been doing their duty, going about our business as they have been doing ever since Valley Forge. Who are and who were these men and women? For our local heroes a brick in the walkway at the Veteran's Memorial may be the only mention, the only memorial that reminds the rest of us that freedom is not free.

CR

**All gave some – Some gave all
Freedom is not free**

Signs of Spring

It seemed to come on all-of-a-sudden this year. There was a false start or two but then the sun and the south wind really swept the scene. A person could almost watch the ice melt on the bayou. Well, maybe you wouldn't really want to sit there and watch but I believe the ice was melting faster than the grass was growing and I've heard people say something about "watching the grass grow."

The coming of the first robin has always been the harbinger of spring. I learned that back in grade school. Robins are nice to see but I haven't seen one yet this spring. Maybe that should be telling me something? I recall, I think it was back in 1992, when the temperature was still down around zero and it was April. Dorothy and I were living in the woods up along the Yellow Dog River back then. When I say in the woods I mean awaaay up in the woods. We were a couple and half miles from the nearest anything. Wood heated the cabin. We had a small propane space heater to carry us through cold nights. The propane tanks were located outside though and it got so cold that winter that the propane wouldn't evaporate. Our little space heater went out. We experienced a couple of pretty frosty mornings back then. As I recall that was about the time momma (Dorothy) suggested

– all you married guys know what a "suggestion" from momma means – that maybe we should move back to our centrally heated, commercially electrified, hot and cold running water with even a telephone in our house on Lakewood Lane. Need I say more?

I think this year it's truly spring though. There may yet be a frosty morning or two but I think winter is over. The robins aren't here yet but we have had a couple other messengers. The other night I opened the door to the porch and was greeted by a familiar chorus of "Spring Peepers." Peepers are little frogs, about the size of your thumb. Some call them tree frogs. They congregate in our marsh each spring. They serenade each other with the same thoughts in mind that are attributed to the rest of us each spring. When it gets a little warmer evenings I'll open the sliding door in the bedroom and let those little peepers sing me to sleep.

Another sure sign of spring scurried across the back porch a couple days ago. Dorothy and I have a couple feeders hanging out on the porch. I don't specify "bird" feeders as we pretty much feed whatever might come along. There are ducks that spend the whole winter up here. I guess they congregate in the open water on the Chocolay River. We scatter whole corn on the ice on the bayou and the ducks come from everywhere. Our sunflower seeds feed several species of birds. Those feeders are hung where they're safe from the squirrels and the nocturnal raccoon that shows up now and then. We do have another feeder next to the porch railing however that the squirrels and raccoons can get to – and they do. We also scatter a few peanuts, still in their shells, on the porch and I swear the blue jays are there to get them before they even hit the ground. In nature it's whoever gets there quickest that eats. Maybe that's where the expression "the quick and the dead" originated?

Those are some of the critters who are with us all winter. Those little harbingers of spring I referred to are the chipmunks. Those little chippies will spend their summers scurrying back and forth between our feeders – and wherever else they go – and their burrow underground. The chippies have a regular apartment down there. Watching them come and go I believe their residence is under a portion of our driveway. They'll haul seeds and feed down into their burrow and store it all in their chipmunk cupboard. Their apartment will have a living/sleeping area and a bathroom area also. Once the cold weather and snow of late fall arrive they'll disappear, retiring to await the next spring. They don't really hibernate as they get up now and then, the familiar bathroom call, to eat a bit and things like that – maybe a little TV? No! I don't think there's anything on television they'd want to watch. There's not that much on TV that interests me either for that matter. I wonder if they get up at night as frequently as I do? No matter. The chipmunks are up and about. Spring is here – fur-shure.

CR

**To cheer yourself
Try cheering up someone else.**

C&R

Beside the Still Waters

Somebody once said, "The best things in life are free," to which some wag might add, "But that was before inflation." We seem to be conditioned early in life to improve, to better ourselves, to "succeed." For many "succeed" seems to be a metaphor for making money or a getting a fancy house or a bigger truck or a faster car. Another philosophical thinker called that "The Rat Race." Then again someone adds that the rats seem to be winning. You can read into that whatever you want.

I don't mean to rain on anyone's parade but I want to suggest that a lot of life might get lost along the way.

Something new has appeal and novelty but it soon wears off. Then we may get something bigger, better, more impressive. Same thing – it wears off.

Maybe these opinions are because I'm getting older – 78 on this next birthday. "Oh, you're just a kid," well-meaning friends say. That's all very nice but I know that I'm a whole lot closer to the end than I am to the beginning. Because of that I try to enjoy each day to its maximum. As long as I keep my weight down and do regular physical exercise life is still good.

Snow recently decorated the trees down toward Sundell with a white sugar-like icing, like cookies. The crews driving the snowplows may not see it that way but you can't change it. You might as well enjoy it.

Have you ever stopped at sunset point on Presque Isle on a summer evening? just as the sun goes down? There's no charge. It's free. It's just as beautiful if you're indecently wealthy or if you're poor as a church mouse. In fact all too often the worry that comes with the weight of worldly possessions detracts from the beauty of the moment. And it is just a brief moment. If you're there, you may see it. If not, well, that's the way it goes.

Do you ever stop to watch the waves roll in? see them wash over the sand or crash onto the rocks or the breakwater? Waves have been doing that for how many billions of years. It hasn't changed. They'll still be doing that long after you and I have passed on.

Next time you're scrubbing down in your shower,

pause, just stand there and appreciate the hot water flowing over you. Enjoy! There's nothing out in the work-a-day world that won't wait an extra couple minutes. Relax! The secret of success is not to take yourself or anything else too seriously. Learn to laugh a lot especially at yourself. You're not going to get out of it alive so enjoy it while you're here.

Here's another thread of philosophical thought to follow. Most of us are familiar with the Judeo-Christian 23rd Psalm. One line reads: ". . . He leadeth me beside the still waters . . ." That line was particularly meaningful to a society of shepherds. Sheep won't drink from moving water. You've got to "leadeth them beside the still waters."

My mother built the home I now live in while I was over in that Viet Nam thing. She named the home "Still Waters." My mother was a lot smarter than I am. I appreciate that more every day.

With each passing New Year I hope you, too, will enjoy each day and find your own "Still Waters."

CR

**Making a living is not the same as
Making a life.**

CR

The Birthday Party

My grandson, Levi Charlebois, just turned six years old. And of course there was a Birthday Party. And what's a party without all your friends? There were kids from his Kindergarten class at Superior Central School in Eben. There were kids from the Chocolay Children's Center in Harvey. There were playmates and cousins and parents and grandparents, it may even have included a couple strangers that just happened to be passing by. There was quite a crowd: 27 children, 26 adults and two pretty near brand new babies.

Did we have to find someone's vacant barn to hold

this celebration? No! There's a place in Marquette that occasionally receives a little publicity but not nearly as much as it should. It's called the Upper Peninsula Children's Museum and it's located in the 100 block of West Baraga Avenue.

There are no big signs sticking out over the street or anything – something to do with the zoning in the area – but the building front advertises the museum quite well. Once you've parked in the ample parking lot you just "follow the yellow brick road" to the entrance. Well the yellow brick road is kind of white this time of year but you won't have any trouble finding it. It'll be yellow again come spring.

There are so many things there for the kids to do and see and experience that they just don't know where to start. They wear themselves out just running from one attraction to another. There are a few eye openers there for parents too. The Children's Museum certainly was the answer for a party the size of Levi's. It was children, showing what they've done and are still doing that have designed and built this museum. The place will amaze you.

Regular in-house programs are designed for toddlers up through eighteen year olds and are interesting for older-than-eighteen adults also. There's a program where little ones learn to stick things together, another where they can learn simple cooking. Or maybe they'll choose to make BIG art works or learn to make a story or to paint. Now before you get that sinking feeling about kids painting you don't have to worry about clean up. The folks at the museum take care of that. There's another program called "Making Noise." I would have guessed that kids were pretty good at that already but this program attempts to introduce rhythm to the noise. Who knows, maybe there's a future Mozart in the group?

Schoolteachers can arrange cooperative classes for their kids in areas of history or a rudimentary introduction to Democratic Values. These are taught through demonstration and role-playing. There is also a program on machinery and how it works and another titled the "Atomic Comic," about your body and why and how it does what it does – or sometimes doesn't.

Mr. Jeff Davis comes by at times bringing his snakes and turtles. He conducts a hands-on lecture where kids can become more knowledgeable and comfortable with these little known and lesser-appreciated creatures that share our planet.

All these attractions are available to everyone. You can visit casually or take advantage of the offer to provide a place and facilities for parties, parties of whatever kind through and including sleepovers. People who live outside the immediate area – or not - can arrange to bus in, have a good time, spend the night at the facility (it has kitchen facilities) in sleeping bags they bring with them, enjoy a breakfast (you must arrange), have an enjoyable morning, and then bus back home. It's hard to beat a deal like that. You've got to include some adults of course to accompany the kids, especially the smaller children, but once they're there just keep out of the children's way.

There's a sign on one of the interactive displays that states, "STOP – ADULTS! Let your children solve most of their own problems!" Parents, pay attention!

At the birthday party I found it a full time job just keeping from getting run down. Kids were excitedly rushing from one display to another and a slow moving adult is apt to get run over. The kids were running - geez! Where's Hudson? Hudson is Levi's younger brother and I'm supposed to be looking after him. Where is he? Maybe he's over piloting that airplane next to the weather station. Or maybe he's a future Karl Bonak learning his craft in the weather station itself. No, no, I seem to remember he was particularly fond of crawling into a stomach and coming out through the large intestine. I watched him do that. His cousin, Miranda, was there too crawling through the heart and sliding down the outer veins. I'd better go - look – while - - what's that questioning expression on your face? You seem to be wondering what I'm talking about. Well, I'm not going to tell you. Go to the Upper Peninsula Children's Museum and find out for yourself.

CR

Trails Gone By

I get up toward Big Bay occasionally and try to make a side trip to our little cabin on the Yellow Dog River. It's pleasant up there, quiet and serene, just me and the wind and the woods with maybe a woodland critter or two wandering by. There are a lot of memories that permeate the whole area.

The place was founded when the original owner, a lumberjack called Tom "Tin Can" Sullivan, decided that he had had enough of this world. He did not "go gentle into that good night" but went out with a blast – literally. He shot himself in the cabin. A bunch of guys from Marquette, including my father, grandfather and uncle, bought the place from his estate, such as it was, and named it "The Yellow Dog Fishing and Hunting Club." Tom had been a loner without family anyone knew of. He was buried in Potter's Field in Marquette's Park View Cemetery. If you're ever up to the cabin alone on a quiet moonlit night you can talk to Tom. He doesn't say much though.

I remember, as a youngster, getting lost up here. I didn't find my way out 'til near dark. It scared me at the time and kind of had my dad worried too. I don't know if he ever did tell mom about that. Of course I didn't say anything. "Macho" guys don't talk about things like that.

Dorothy and I once lived up here, year around, for a couple or three years. We built a small "guest house" six or eight hundred feet south of the cabin for when our kids stopped by. That's where I'm writing this. The place sits on a south facing ridge with a beautiful view of a small valley. I remember one deer hunting season "back in the ole days." One of the club members had seated himself against a tree overlooking the valley to watch for deer. It was a pleasant fall afternoon with good visibility as a light fall of snow had covered the ground. Sitting in the warm sun he nodded off to sleep. Another one of the guys, returning from his hunting, came upon him and woke him up. There, in the fresh snow not twenty feet from him, were a set of fresh deer tracks. He was awhile living that down.

Then, the day I was born in 1929, November 15,

the first day of deer season, my dad rushed up to the camp to tell grandpa his first grandchild had been born. Grandpa had been in to Big Bay and, using one of the three phones in town back then, had learned of the event. When dad arrived and before he could say anything grandpa held up his hand and said, "We know, Ben, we know all about it."

My dad stopped in surprise and asked, "How did you find out?"

Grandpa turned and, pointing to the wall said, "They called on the phone."

There on the wall was an old (brand new for the time) telephone, battery operated with a hand crank to call the operator. Just then the phone rang. Grandpa picked up the receiver, put it to his ear and spoke into the trumpet mouthpiece. "Hello. Ben? Yeah he's here, just got here. I'll put him on." He handed the ear piece to dad.

Dad, in amazement, took the phone and spoke into the trumpet. "Hello? Hello?" Everybody was grinning and it dawned on him. There was no telephone up there. This was a rigged deal engineered by my grandfather. Dad lived with that for a while too. "There's a phone call for you, Ben." I still have that old telephone.

These memories are why the old cabin is more than just a piece of property on the Yellow Dog River. It's a piece of my life. But everything changes. Driving in just now I couldn't help but notice that the old two-rut logging trail is now a well worn road, a woods road but a very passable one. There are several new cabins along the way. Cabins? There's a place going up in the middle of the woods just west of Bear Lake that's as big as a basketball court. There's a couple living a quarter mile west with a work shop where they build – I don't know – rustic furniture I guess. Another couple with young children lives just a quarter mile to the north. On the way in I passed a side road with an "in town" type street sign: "Suzuki Trail,"

No, things sure aren't what they used to be. But I can remember the way they were. That'll never change.

CR

When You're All Alone

It's five o'clock Saturday morning. No one is up but me. The sun hasn't begun to show yet. It's dark. The thermometer on the outside railing registers eight degrees below zero. And that's here on the lakeshore. It's probably colder farther inland. The weather sure has changed in a couple short days.

I'm going to slip outside to get the morning paper. As soon as I step out the door the cold hits. Snow squeaks underfoot. When the snow squeaks, well, that thermometer wasn't lying. A wave of regret washes over me for not having slipped into a heavier coat and cap. If there were any wind, even a slight breeze I would probably have gone back to suit up a bit more. Instead I just stand there. It's cold! It's still! It's quiet as a grave. Everything seems frozen in time, motionless, nothing moves. Time stands still. There's only a hundred feet or so to get to the newspaper box. I guess can make that OK.

The moon has just passed its full stage but it's still big and bright. The sky is clear, dark indigo - almost black. A pine tree branch and needles stand out in sharp silhouette against the broad blue-white face of the moon. Even in that intense cold the sight stops me in my tracks. It's beautiful! I wonder if anyone else is looking at it? A couple lines of long-ago read poetry come to mind: "Have you ever been out in the great alone when the moon is bright and clear? And the icy mountains hem you in with a silence you 'most could hear?"

The cold relentlessly seeps in intruding on my reverie. I shiver and get moving again. I'll grab the newspaper and get back inside, back beside that warm fireplace in the house. And the paper's not there! I think to myself, "Goodness gracious my-oh-my" (Words to that effect). Maybe the guy who delivers the paper is standing somewhere staring at that moon too. There's ice everywhere. My footing is something less than certain. Care is the watchword.

Once I'm back inside the radiant heat from the open fireplace feels doubly warm. With my back to the fire I spread my hands to soak up as much warmth as possible. Then I turn around to "toast" both sides evenly. As I stand there, bathed in the luxury of that radiant heat it's doubly appreciated after exposure to the bitter cold outside. This brief luxury is one of the true pleasures of life. So many of us don't seem aware, don't take time to enjoy these moments. Too many of us are in a rush to – to what? To material things we think are more important.

As a person gets older – and I have – how many times we look back with regret, regret for not having spent more time with our children when they were little for example. And how many times was that moon up there silhouetting that tree branch - and I didn't see it? I do remember many open fires along the way though, the heat from which I absorbed, the camaraderie around which I enjoyed. Those memories are relived each time I repeat the experience. I wonder if my son or daughters remember the good times, the times we – ah, well, those are days gone by. As my wife, Dorothy, tells me, ". . . you can't go forward in life until you let go of your past failures and heartaches." Hopefully they weren't all failures but some memories cause heartache anyway. I guess I've been fortunate, in my life, to know ladies who were – and are – smarter than I am. Oh, well, back to the future!

Often at night I awaken and get up in the cold, in the dark, and fumble my way to the bathroom. That's another of the features that comes with age. If you don't yet know that, you will. I have learned when I get up to pull the blankets back over the bed. When I return – and it doesn't take long –I raise the blanket and am able slide into a spot still warm from my having been there. That's another of life's little pleasures. You learn not to leave the sheets exposed to grow cold and chill you as you crawl back into bed. Warming your self in front of an open fire. Pausing under a hot shower to just stand there and enjoy the sensation. Kneel down, get down to the child's level, and let a grandson or granddaughter give you a big sincere hug. I don't mean a "duty" hug for grandpa but a sincere "I love you" hug. If you're not experiencing these things in your life, you're not living you simply exist.

If you can beat the stock market, move mountains, change the world someway; history will appropriately record the event. Your personal life however might leave a memory like that hole that stays in the water after you remove your finger. It's all these little pleasures in life that add up, that are important. These little things are what make up who you are and how those you love will remember you. In the end, what else matters?

◌

You Are What You Eat

Ms. Mary Charlebois, RD (Registered Dietician), teaches Chocolay Children's Center Children good nutrition – before it becomes a problem.

March is National Nutrition Month. I'll bet most of you didn't even know that? As you go about your daily life it's improbable that you'll see anyone you think might be suffering from malnutrition. Well look again. Just because the many of us, and "many" is rapidly growing to be a large majority, are overweight, obese – Obese! You know, like not being able to see your own shoes anymore. But all that flab doesn't mean we're not malnourished. We just aren't getting the proper foods. It's "we," not "society" or the "fast-food-chains," that are gorging ourselves on "junk food." This addiction to easy access to brief sensory pleasure, to a momentary oral satisfaction costs much more than the 99 cents we pay for a quarter-pounder with fries. The greatest price is the severe downgrade in the quality of our lives. I would have said "the 'long term' quality of life" but an advantage, if you want to call it that, is that your life is probably going to be a lot shorter. Ah but in keeping with the positive theme of Natural Nutrition Month I won't harp on that. Let's keep our focus positive, on nutrition.

Allow me a little aside here if you will. Some people work solely for monetary return; to make a living they'll tell you. While making a living is not a trivial matter it's also important that a person enjoy what they do. Their job should give them social interaction, pleasure, a sense of fulfillment. It's what Humanistic Behavioral Psychologist Abraham Maslow called "self-actualization." With a title like "Humanistic Behavioral Psychologist" talking, pay attention. Self-actualization is a feeling of accomplishment above and beyond survival and existence. It's what a person gets in addition to making a living. It's when they feel they're doing something they want to do instead of something they have to do to get by. If they enjoy what they do, they'll be devoted to the task. They'll do it well. They'll extend themselves to excel not for approval and praise but because they get a feeling of accomplishing something worth while. Now let me try to tie this all together for you.

A group of Dietitians at Marquette General Hospital were talking about March being National Nutrition

Month. They were wondering what they might be able to do for the occasion. One of them suggested maybe they could take a half-day or so and talk to students in area schools about proper nutrition. Many of you might feel that a lecture on nutrition ranks right up there with a dental root canal experience. If that's your reaction, look around at your fellow citizens – or just climb on a scale yourself? It's away beyond time we (and that includes you and me) did something about nutritional health.

With the approval of Carol Holman, head of the Dietetic Department at Marquette General Hospital, each of these eight dietary professionals, Registered Dieticians all, selected a school within the Marquette-Alger-Delta-County area. They arranged to speak to children, to grade school classes in selected schools on proper nutrition.

Ms. Mary Charlebois spoke to the kids at the Chocolay Children's Center in Harvey. These were probably some of the youngest children who received this presentation but Mary did an outstanding job with displays, explanations and examples. A child's attention span is not very long you know and lecturing them is kind of like herding cats. With the support of Children's Center owner Ms. Lisa Bera and the gentle, able assistance of her capable staff the children learned about the food pyramid, the benefits of eating natural wholesome foods and the penalties of too much – too much – well, let's just call it "junk food."

These dedicated ladies from the Marquette General

Hospital's Dietetic Department are to be commended for their efforts above and beyond the call of their jobs, for reaching out to address a problem that is nation wide and growing. But all this dedicated effort isn't going to work without the active support of you, you parents out there. Inquire about what your children have learned. Support them by providing healthful and nutritious meals, by teaching them good eating habits. It doesn't mean that a hamburger and fries along with a little time in that alluring children's playroom can't be indulged in on a special occasion but learn about the food pyramid yourself. You'll not only be building a happier healthier future for your children but you'll be helping yourself to a better life while doing it.

CR

A Job Well Done

As we wander down the road of life, trying to be happy, trying to enjoy each day there's something that we all too often overlook. We would all like to have the admiration and respect of our peers. We want to be recognized in some way for some of the things we have done. And, of course, we hope folks don't spend too much time looking at those things we might not have done so well. The world may not notice whether we do good or ill but, when all is said and done, what counts is what we, each one of us, thinks of ourselves.

Are you happy with yourself? Really down-deep happy or are you busy explaining why you did or didn't do this or that or whatever? Are you following me in this? I'm talking about you, you close up and personal. I'm talking about what you, down deep where nobody sees, think of yourself. You can state reasons (excuses) explaining why (or why not) you did (or didn't) do thus and so. Maybe it's just losing weight or exercising more or – make your own list. Everyone knows these things are harder to do than they are to talk about. People listening to your explanation will nod sympathetically and agree. That's the easiest, the most "politically correct" thing for a listener to do. And it'll "keep peace in the family." What good would it do if they said, "You're full of x*#.

Get off your butt and DO it." They may think that but people who come out and say it, well, they probably don't expect to be invited back any time soon. Of all the things people can say that can hurt you, it's often when they speak the truth that it can hurt the most.

There are examples everywhere of folks who grit their teeth, suck in their bellies and just do it. So can the rest of us! We can all "just do it!" We're all cut from the same cloth, made from the same pattern. We've all got the same tools. Don't explain, just DO it!

Maybe this'll help. It's a little thing titled "Invictus" written by Wm. E. Henley:

> "Out of the night which covers me
> Black as the pit from pole to pole
> I thank whatever gods may be
> For my unconquerable soul.
> In the fell clutch of circumstance
> I have not winced nor cried aloud.
> Beneath the bludgeonings of chance
> My head, though bloody, is unbowed.
> Beyond this place of wrath and tears
> Looms but the horror of the shade
> Yet the menace of the passing years
> Finds, and shall find me unafraid.
> It matters not how strait the gate
> How charged with punishment the scroll
> I am the master of my fate
> I am the Captain of my soul."
>   **William Ernest Henley**

On the brighter side of this ledger, once you've succeeded the sense of accomplishment is tremendous. You no longer have to explain anything to anybody. You're strengthened, uplifted, self confident. A couple positive accomplishments and you're convinced of your ability to handle anything that comes along life's road.

Don't start by trying to establish world peace but set up smaller more easily attainable goals. If losing weight is your thing, don't try to lose fifteen pounds the first week. Don't even try to lose five pounds or any weight at all. First set a goal of not eating – nothing at all – after six PM every night. You don't have to do this forever. Just do it for one night – tonight. Then do it tomorrow night. When you've got this working for a couple weeks – and this next may be a little harder – don't eat anything between meals. It'll work! Believe me. I've been there.

And stay away from pills and patches and potions. They're another form of "Excuse." I think it was Socrates or one of those "deep thinkers" who said "In every medicine there is a little poison." Let 'em alone if you can!

Just look around at your fellow citizens and you'll see – well – you know what you'll see. You know they aren't happy that way. We can point fingers at "fast food" and make all sorts of explanations but it's us, you and me, who put that food in our mouths.

This next is a little known secret: Get up from the table while you still feel a bit hungry. A half an hour later you won't feel hungry. It works if you'll just DO it.

When you're a couple months or so into "Doctor Mukkala's" handy dandy feel better, gain self confidence and change your life plan, climb on a scale. Surprise! You won't even have to climb on a scale, you'll know. To celebrate your success, splurge. Go have an ice cream cone – just one dip and just this one time. Then back to the good fight. You can do it! "You are the master of your fate. You are the Captain of your soul."

◌

What Are You Worth?

"What people earn" was the headline on the cover of a recent issue of "Parade," the magazine insert in Sunday newspapers. There were pictures of people, their names, ages, occupations, where they worked and their annual income. The assumption was that money was the measure of each person's worth. That seems a universally accepted measure of a person but is that really what they're worth? Stop and think about that for a minute. If what a person is "worth" is measured by a cold figure on a bank statement I think the boat has sailed without them.

We seem to be conditioned from a very young age to view a person's value by how much money they have. We assume they have fewer worries than the rest of us and are happier. The idea is accepted like a religion – by faith. "Seek ye an occupation with a generous monetary compensation," we are told, "and you will live happily ever after." But is that true? Let's talk about that.

Along life's road I've known people who were rich, very rich. They had money, property, material wealth but were they happy? Some seemed to be but I don't think they were any happier than you or I. About half of them (maybe more, I'm being conservative here) had a whole lot more worries than I did. More than just a few of them were in need of psychiatric help.

Let me tell you about one particular fella. I was in the Air Force at the time, a pilot, stationed in Texas. This guy was a civilian. He owned several patents and a factory that built earth augers. I never knew there was so much to making holes in the ground 'til I met him. I was single in those days and lived in a barracks. He'd call me of an evening, especially if he'd been hitting the sauce a bit – and he did that quite frequently. When I'd answer the phone he'd say, "Hi, Ace! Come-a-runnin'" and he'd hang up. I'd drive over to his home, a large ranch-style home on several acres of land. It was surrounded by woods, had a three car attached garage, a fishing pond with a swimming area, a patio and a well manicured lawn. It was quite an impressive place.

This particular evening his wife's unmarried sister had stopped by unexpectedly. I guess I was invited as company for her. She was good people, nice looking and a pleasant personality. The evening was going quite well. The fella had been pretty well oiled when he called me and he hadn't slowed up any since. We were sitting in their den area talking. During a break in the conversation he turned, raised his head looked at us and spewed out some of the vilest language I've ever heard anywhere. He wasn't saying anything other than mouthing this filth. In the shocked silence that followed this outburst he pitched forward on his face on the floor, passed out cold, dead drunk. He was a big, overweight guy and it took all three of us to haul him into the bedroom and roll him into bed.

His wife was shocked and embarrassed. She stuttered and stammered trying to understand and explain what had just happened. Her sister and I attempted to make light of it for her sake. The evening had pretty much ended.

The next time I saw the guy he seemed his old self. He appeared to have no recollection of that evening. No one else spoke of it. Yeah, that guy was rich but do you think he was happy? Do you think his wife was happy? I don't know enough about psychiatry or his family situation to even pretend to guess what was eating at him. With all his money would you want to trade places with him? If his picture and income had been listed in the Parade magazine would that dollar figure be a true measure of his worth? Of what he had earned in his life?

Riches, real wealth is not measured in dollars. I paraphrase Ralph Waldo Emerson: "Who has lived well, who laughs often deep and long, who has the respect of intelligent people and the love of children; who leaves the world a better place than they found it by way of a healthy child, a garden patch or a redeemed social condition; who never lacked an appreciation of beauty nor failed to express it; who looked for the best in others and gave the best they had. If even one life has breathed easier because of them, their worth is without measure."

CR

Follow your dream.

ℜ

Guys With White Hats

The old western movies still get shown on television now and then. I'm a sucker for those old movies even if it's in the middle of the night. I usually record them to watch the next day. What I'm talking about here are the reeeelly old ones, with Randolph Scott and Hopalong Cassidy and, of course, John Wayne - guys like that. Back then you knew right away who the "good guys" were. They were the fellas who wore the white hats. The bad guys wore dark colors, and sullen expression and were mostly ugly. They weren't necessarily ugly actors but the make-up people made them ugly anyway.

Another fact about those early films was that the good guys always won. I don't mean that in the context of a steamy scene with the film's female lead, heavy breathing and each one trying to swallow the other one's tongue. Some times, in the "modern" movies, they seem to have designs on the whole head. Anyway that's what it looks like. In the more discreet films the camera may fade away, maybe to a white hat hanging on the door. If they had done that other back in the old days I think we kids at the Saturday matinee would have rioted. No, the accepted ending back then was the hero fondly scratching his faithful horse's ears then mounting up and riding slowly into the sunset. There were vicious rumors spread by a lunatic fringe about the hero kissing his horse. We kids could probably have accepted that. No "tongue sucking" though.

I don't know if it was a movie-making law back in those days or just good judgment on the part of producers but I still think it was a good policy. In the end, the good guys always win. It set an example for us young and impressionable kids. I wonder what impressions the kid's are getting these days?

Even though I've seen this movie many times and know the outcome isn't going to change, I still enjoy watching Wyatt Earp cleaning up Tombstone, Arizona. It all culminates in the shoot out at the OK corral. Ole Wyatt really did the job! Now I'm going to let you in on a little secret. This is a little known fact that I'll bet a lot, I'll even bet even that almost all of you don't know. We in the U.P. had a "Wyatt Earp" of our own. This happened a while ago, not a reeelly long time ago but awhile. The "hero" involved in this "clean up" is still alive and walks among us. I'm not going to tell you the fella's name though – lawsuits and all, you know - but I will tell you the story. It all took place in the quiet little town of Big Bay just up the road from Marquette. This was "back in the days of yesteryear."

It happened on a quiet summer afternoon. A group of "wild and lawless" bikers, motorcyclists, descended upon the peaceful law abiding settlement of Big Bay. These weren't the guys from our local motorcycle club. Our local group, among other beneficial acts, strongly supports Bay Cliff Health Camp. Anyone supporting Bay Cliff has my whole hearted backing for almost anything they might do short of outright murder. No, these were out-of-towners, probably a bunch of "apple knockers" from down state, you know, "below the bridge."

Motorcycles were roaring around the streets of town that day disrupting an otherwise peaceful afternoon. They were terrifying mothers with young children. Big Bay wasn't large enough to have a police department but they did have a constable, a lone enforcer of the law of the land. The word went out! There was great need of the "Marshal of Tombstone" – well – it was for the constable but bear with me here. The "shoot out" was destined to take place where the "wild bunch" was hanging out - Perkin's Park - Big Bay's OK Corral!

The fearless Constable boldly confronted the rough and ragged looking group. He identified himself as "the law north of Marquette." He further advised them that there attitude and activities were not acceptable in the peaceable little village of Big Bay. If they wished to be welcome in Big Bay they'd have to "hang up their guns" (reduce their throttle settings) back at the township line. Furthermore, this day they had overstayed their welcome: "Be out of town by sundown!" Actually he said be gone by 6:00 PM but it sounds better the other way.

That confrontation shook the ne'r-do-wells suitably. They left Dodge – er – I mean Big Bay. But the story doesn't end there.

The bikers "left town before sunset" but being of a generation that files a lawsuit at the spill of hot coffee in their own lap, they sought help from a higher authority: they went to the Sheriff in Marquette. They were seeking redress for this affront to their rights and their dignity.

The Sheriff, exercising a combination of authority and diplomacy, was able to smooth over the situation and sent them on their way. He did feel it necessary to discuss the situation with ole Wyatt Earp though. "Geez, XXX, you can't be tellin' people they have to get out of town by sunset." The answer he received would have made even the original Wyatt Earp proud: "It worked, didn't it?"

Those of you who are curious can ask around. Maybe you can discover who "Wyatt Earp" really is but I'm not going to tell you. No sir! I'm not going to say a word. And I also make it a practice to be out of Big Bay by sundown.

☙

Can We Go Fishin'?

"Granpa, can we go fishin'?" He's seven years old.
He's looking at me hopefully with his big blue eyes.

Granpa just melts. I had been working on something important of course - a consultation problem for our President. I was going to advise him on the pros and cons of the use of nuclear weapons in negotiation with Iran. And then too to discuss whether or not to assassinate Hugo Chavez down in Venezuela - making it appear the doings of others of course. The President may have need of my counsel and, looking at the polls, I suspect he might but something more important has come up. My Grandson has asked me, "Granpa, can we go fishin'?"

The future of the world is looking at me through those big blue eyes. Whether or not we go fishin' may not decide nuclear war but then again, in the future, who can tell? What does or doesn't shape a person's character, their empathy, their view of the world? Watching the news the past few days I can't help but notice the contrast between some of our well publicized Hollywood celebrities. On the one hand are those who flaunt the law as if it really doesn't apply to them. On the other hand we have another well known individual who went to Hurricane ravaged Louisiana, financed the project himself and physically worked himself to try to help folks who were less fortunate. Why are these people so different from one another? Who, how and what, along the way, molded the diverse character of those folks? What was the motivator that determined their actions?

The single most important job in this world, bar none, is raising our children. The ladies have rattled their cage about equality and I agree with them. They're demanding equal pay for equal work and recognition for what they are able to do in this world and they're right. But never forget, all you ladies, that you are already the Chief Executive Officer of the most critically important job there is: the raising, nurturing, teaching and shaping of the character of our children. We guys should be involved too of course. Some fathers are better at this than others but we should all try to do the best we can. But ladies never forget it's "the hand that rocks the cradle that rules the world." Kids know this instinctively. When they skin their knee it's momma they turn to.

We make a big thing about our "rights." What gets overlooked is that inherent with every "right" comes a responsibility. Those who claim their "right" to steam up the windows of a parked car (metaphorically speaking) must also accept the responsibility of the result of all that steam. Whoever brings a child into this world, both the gal AND the guy, must accept the responsibility of caring for that child, seeing that the child receives its "rights." A child has a right to two loving, caring parents, to guidance, to an education and to a proper send-off into adulthood. We're very good at demanding our rights. We seem to be equally adept at dodging or evading our responsibilities. My "Chief of Staff," Jud Cole, up in Dollar Bay would say, "When I am the King all this is going to change." Irresponsible daddies – and mommas too – will either fulfill their obligations or "off mit the heads." Well, enough about my future political campaign. Election for King is still a few months off.

Grandparents, including volunteer substitute grand-parents, are unique. They have – or should have – fewer job and career demands placed upon them than parents do. We have more free time to devote to the kids. We, all we grandparents out there, have the opportunity to talk to grandchildren from a wealth of experience. Realize though that there's a difference between talking TO children and talking AT them. Somebody once told me that the best sermons are not preached. Think about that. It doesn't just apply to preachers. The kids may or may not hear what you say but they never fail to see what you do. Which do you think makes the greater impression, the talk? Or the action? If you plant weeds in your garden, you can shout "potatoes" all day but weeds are what's going to grow, weeds are what you're going to harvest. Those kids are the future, our future too.

"Can we go fishin'?" You bet your boots we can! The President and all those less important matters will just have to wait.

CR

Cassandra Complex

"Be reasonable! Do it my way!" That's a thought many of we – we – should I say "Senior Citizens"? have when dealing with more junior members of society.

Time goes by and the world changes. Many of us have a longing for "the good old days" but only seem to remember the best of the good old days. Much has gotten better. Other areas, well, we could argue for quite some time over whether they got better or worse. There are things we oldsters have learned that seem fundamental – no! - They don't just "seem" they ARE fundamental. These are things that a person finally recognizes after a lifetime of having it pounded into them. The frustration arises when we try to tell younger folks what we have learned. That's where the "Cassandra" thing comes in. Let me tell you about Cassandra.

Cassandra was a desirable young lady back in the days of Greek mythology. The god Apollo was smitten and was trying to win her favor. Back in those days the gods were like corporate executives and used to fraternize with the mere mortals on a regular basis. To gain Cassandra's favor Apollo gave her the gift of foresight, Cassandra could see the future. Unfortunately Cassandra spurned Apollo's advances. Apollo was not happy.

One of the rules was that once a god gave a gift,

they couldn't take it back. What could he do? Since he couldn't take the "foresight" thing back, he simply added the condition that no one would believe her. Do you see where I'm going with this?

Much of what we oldsters tell the youngsters may fall in that category. Some of what we say "ain't necessarily so." Maybe it doesn't fit in the changing times. But there are some things that are fundamental, that are basic, that are true. We "old fogies" didn't realize them when we were young either. Here's why I think that happens: When you're young you're tentatively feeling your way into a strange new world. Self-image is super important. A young person's self-esteem is as fragile as a soap bubble. The tendency is to protect it by lashing out viciously at anything, real or imagined, or anybody that seems to threaten it. Get over it! The only person who can put you down is you! Some people, even as they grow older never seem to grasp that fact.

A couple comments recently forwarded to me by my friend, Al Denton, are worth paraphrasing here. These are revelations that come with age: to cheer yourself up, cheer up someone else; recognize that making a living as not the same as making a life; whatever you do in life treat other people, not necessarily as they treat you but the way you want them to treat you.

Another of the things age teaches. Your search for happiness will never succeed until you realize this: by bringing a little happiness to someone else you'll be repaid many times over in the happiness that comes to you. This will happen even though no one, including the person or persons you helped may ever know what you did.

Here's another senior secret. A person doesn't have to "know it all." How refreshing it would be if politicians, instead of talking 'round and 'round without ever answering a question, would simply say, "I don't know - but I'll find out." A teacher I had along the way once told me, "The first indication that you're learning anything at all is when you realize how much there is that you don't know." By that measure you're presently reading the words of a genius.

Let me close my sermon with these thoughts: "Please," "Thank you," "You're welcome," "Excuse me," and "I'm sorry." Whether you realize it or not being polite doesn't diminish your stature. It increases it. The older and I would add wiser, folks know you gain admiration and respect with those words.

Courtesy, as demonstrated by the use of those phrases, is the lubricant that smoothes the daily flow of human interaction. They'll add mileage to any relationship. Try it! It doesn't cost a thing. Take a moment to hold a door open for a lady or a senior citizen. "Thank you." "You're welcome." First thing you know you're feeling better about who you are. Happiness just naturally comes around. Maybe these were some of the things Cassandra was trying to tell people? Think about that – and don't you fall victim to Apollo's second condition.

CR

To thine own self be true
And it shall follow,
As the night follows day,
You cannot then be false to anyone
Wm. Shakespeare

The Mirror

The world we live in is a mirror. Do you believe that? What you see in that mirror is a reflection of yourself. The world will reflect the attitude, the "face" you are showing it. I've got to admit there are some, call them "smudges" on that mirror. Some are people whose own "mirror" is almost completely obscured, negative because that's the way they think. Let's accept that and leave them to the psychiatrist. Unfortunately those people smudge your mirror but realize that it's them, that's their personality not your reflection. If there are too many smudges you should examine yourself and maybe find new friends? Let me explain that a little more.

I believe it was Jerry Reed, the country singer who used to say, "He who expecteth nuthin' ain't gonna be disappointed." That flip phrase resonates with too many of us. Some of you probably don't know Jerry Reed. No matter. Pay attention to what he said. His remark insinuates that a person is not going to get anywhere anyway so forget about it. What I'm going to try to convince you of is that you make your own life and that "mirror" I'm referring to is showing you what it is. You'll see yourself in that mirror.

Here's a little story that exemplifies that idea: There was a little boy, oh, maybe six or eight years old. He had to be one of the world's greatest optimists. To him everything looked wonderful. His parents worried that the shock of disappointment was going to happen sooner or later and they wanted to be there to protect him from this trauma. For his birthday one year, instead of the electric train which he wanted, they piled horse dung on the floor of his room. When he came home from school that day they told him his birthday present was in his room. He gleefully ran up the stairs. The parents waited, ready to console him. Nothing! They waited a bit longer. Still nothing! Finally they went up to his room and opened the door. The little boy was happily throwing handfuls of dung this way and that. "What are you doing?" his father asked. The little boy looked up with a smile and said, "With all this manure, there must be a pony in here someplace." He wasn't seeing any smudges.

Nothing you or I say or do here is going stop the Iraqis' from blowing up their children and each other. People in Mexico are looking for a better life than they find in their own country. They want to come to the United States. You and I can't do anything about that either. There may be folks locally who have fallen upon hard times. We can do something about that. Local charities, St. Vincent DePaul or the Salvation Army are set up for that and we can help by helping them. Maybe we can get involved in a local assistance project. That's going to make your mirror a whole lot brighter. These are things we can and should do rather than just talking about them.

On the other hand sitting around bemoaning things we can't change or correct just shovels gloom and doom onto everybody within hearing distance. Pretty soon you'll find there is no one within hearing distance. You'll be sitting all alone. That's what you'll see in that mirror I'm talking about. We each have the ability to brighten our own little corner of the world. We're looking at our own reflection that's being projected on the world around us.

Who do you like to be around? Aren't they the happy, positive thinking folks with the "can do" attitude? We all know there are crooked politicians and bad things happening. We should also know that there are hard working honest politicians and many good things happening. Do as much as you can to remedy what you can but don't get down and roll in the mud just to roll in the mud.

It was Henry Ford who said, "If you think you can – or if you think you can't – you're probably right." The emphasis is on who you see in that mirror. That's who folks around you are seeing and living with every day. If you wish you could avoid what you see there, they probably do too – and they will.

CR

The biggest obstacle in your life
Looks back at you from the mirror.

CR

Take The Road Less Traveled

"Two roads diverged in a wood and I, I took the one less traveled by and that's made all the difference." I was talking with a young fella the other day about which road to take in life, about what is and what's not important.

For many young folks their eye is on money. They wish to be millionaires – "billionaires" these days, I guess. That has great influence on their choice. Ah, but the question you should ask yourself is, is the money worth it? Look beyond that illusory facade represented by the term "money." It's not really the money you want. It's what we're led to believe that money will achieve. It appears to offer comfort, security, "toys" and power. These seem to be the rewards of material possessions. Is that what you want your life to be about?

I had better make a full disclosure of my own position here: the IRS isn't apt to be auditing my tax return. It would hardly be worth the price of the postage. But my life, I believe, with all its ups and downs, has been and still is a pretty good run. So here are "Doctor Mukkala's" handy dandy suggestions for happiness at no charge to you - and worth every penny you pay.

First, get an education. There is so much out there in this modern world you should know a little bit about, a lot of it before deciding what to do. Besides, you can't make all the mistakes in the world – there's not time. Learn from the mistakes made by those who have gone before. You get the fundamentals of life and living in kindergarten through grade 12. If you paid attention that's a foundation on which the rest of your life can be built. If your interest has been peaked you may want more education. Go for it. The choice is yours and the time is now. I recommend it but, for one reason or another, we can't all do that.

Secondly explore the options you have available. Concentrate on things you enjoy, things you like to do. You'll be selecting what you'll be spending a whole lot of your life doing so choose carefully. You'll be happier earning beans and bacon in a job you enjoy doing than making a million dollars working at the thing Uncle Charlie told you to do because "There's a lot of money there."

The Christian Bible – and for this example don't think of it as "sacred religious text" but think of it as a book of philosophy - doesn't say, "Money is the root of all evil." The correct quotation is "the love of money is the root of all evil." Beware the spin-doctors in our lives that seem to promise "pie in the sky by and by." The glitter of money may seem to make a prospective wife or husband attractive but hearken to another philosophical witticism: "Who marries for money will earn that money." Think about that during a long quiet evening.

We have also become worshippers of personal appearance. "Anorexia Nervosa." is a condition where a person fears weight gain and tries to mimic spindly models in fashion magazines. People literally starve themselves striving for that warped idea of perfection. Cosmetology is a multi billion-dollar industry. Tummy tucks and face-lifts and liposuction are too often desperate attempts to grasp at the fleeting bird of youth and physical appearance. No one can forever maintain that nebulous and transient image of a perfect or near perfect man or woman. Isn't that desperation a lack of self-confidence, a lack of belief in oneself? Is it what we think we really are that we're trying to conceal? We worship physical beauty, an ethereal thing that's only skin deep at best, transient and much of it is artificial.

True beauty is much deeper, away down beneath any powder and paint. Beauty springs from a person's character, their mind, their heart, deep within their soul. It's empathy, understanding and caring about others. As a person looks back the things recalled with the most pleasure are those things we have done that brought pleasure and happiness to others. These are the things that, combined, form a personality. All the muscle building parlors or expensive beauty salons with their miracles of cosmetology cannot create that which is truly beautiful.

Let me conclude with this: deciding who to marry, who you select to spend your life with is the most important decision you will ever make. Don't be dazzled by glitz and glamour and outward show. When you and your mate grow old, when the joys of discovery and the transient glory of youth have faded and are naught but memories, you'll still have each other. You'll want to be able to talk, to relate, to empathize, to confide in and to understand each another. Those are the times when the mind, the heart, the soul, the personality are exposed as the things that are genuine, true and lasting. When you fall in love, those are the traits you should fall in love with. You're only on this earth for a few years. The one you pick to share them can determine if they are happy years – or an interminable eternity.

"Two roads diverged in a wood and I, I took the one less traveled by and that's made all the difference."

CR

Do The Right Thing

Why do some people "do the right thing," at least in the minds of many of us, while others "do the wrong thing," again according to a lot of us? Is it "nature" or "nurture"? The disagreements over that argument rage on. If your momma tends to be a flibberty-gibbet and your daddy is a bum, chances are you're not going to grow up to be an Albert Einstein. But is that because of something you've inherited from your parent's gene pool or is it because of the watch-me-and-learn home environment you've grown up in? Think about that as you read on.

Big Bay has a small newspaper, "The Bay Independent." Maybe it should call it a pamphlet? It comes out once a month - usually. I'm one of their regular readers. I'm also a little prejudiced toward Big Bay, a fact that, if you didn't know it before, you'll probably gather the idea from this article.

An inner headline in a recent Bay Independent read, "Doing the Right Thing." It's the story of a couple of young Big Bay school kids who, while attending a sporting event, found a rather large sum of money. It was not so much money that it would cause someone to lose the mortgage on the homestead but it was more than loose change in your pocket. They turned the money in to the event security department. It eventually found its way to the grateful victim of the loss. How many of us would have just stuffed the money into our pocket figuring "finder's keepers, loser's weepers"?

The two kids involved subsequently received the admiration of their peers and the adults involved and, appropriately, voluntary gifts from admirers and from the person whose loss they recovered. It was the right thing to do and they did it. Why?

I have a little personal knowledge of some of the people involved with those kids. Some of the folks are teachers at the Powell Township Public School. One child's mother glued my split chin back together as I lay on a restaurant table one afternoon. You're going to have to find out who she was on your own. I'm not going to say any more about that.

The point is that the parents of those kids can stand tall and walk proud also. I further believe that it was a combination of nature and nurture that resulted in those kids "doing the right thing." Raising children is a lot like baking a cake or building something. It takes the proper material, the proper ingredients and in the correct proportions. And it's got to be assembled, mixed, constructed with love and caring. It takes time and more than just a little effort.

Maybe it's because Big Bay is a small town where life moves at a slower pace and everybody knows everybody else and their children. Maybe that's why everyone in a village is a bit closer than, say, the tenants in a high-rise apartment in the fast-moving atmosphere of the pressure-cooker lifestyle that can exist in a big city? People can be so intent on their own lives that they don't even know who lives next door. Maybe it does take a village to raise a child? Whatever it takes it would seem Big Bay has a good share of it. Instead of the current cry to bring industry to Big Bay maybe they need a measure of Big Bay added to industry?

In addition to the village helping raise the child it's the parents, both of them who show a child the way. Kids who only have one parent aren't doomed but they do have a much tougher row to hoe. The relationship between parents and teachers is important too. Each strengthens the role of the other in molding that forming human being that will shape the future of the village, the country, the world. It's increasingly important as kids grow bigger, older and wiser that they know about "doing the right thing." My mother used to say, "There are givers and there are takers. The takers may eat better but the givers sleep better."

I didn't tell you who those kids were, did I? I'm not going to tell you either. Take a ride up to Big Bay. Ask around. Learn the story for yourself. You might check out Bay Cliff Health Camp while you're at it. There's a whole lot of doing the right thing going on out there too. Check it out. You might discover something you can take home and put to good use. What you discover can raise your life and make your whole day brighter.

CR

To whom much is given,
much is required.

☙

What We Eat – and How and When and Why

"You are what you eat!" How many times have you heard that? Quips like that live so long because there's a barb of truth to them. They insinuate without helping. So, is this going to be an "aren't you a bad overweight person" article? I hope not. You look it over and decide. Obviously starvation is not our biggest (no pun intended) national problem.

America's businesses operate on free market principals. We are each free to purchase and consume whatever we wish as long as it's not illegal. Businesses are free to seduce us in any way they can. The result is that we, the people, tend to forego good taste in favor of what tastes good.

I'm fortunate to be blessed with a step-daughter who is a nutritionist and a wife who conscientiously reads labels. I, on the other hand, am a product of the great depression. Those were days when many people weren't able to get enough to eat. "Clean your plate" was the rule at our house. "Think of the poor, starving . . . " I don't remember who was starving but it seems there's always someone.

Whenever I'm away from the protective care of

wife and daughter I face a three-pronged dilemma: 1) Restaurant food is designed to tantalize the taste buds. 2) Servings can only be described as gigantic. 3) My great-depression conditioning demands that I "clean my plate."

So what can those of you do who don't have the benefit of a family nutritionist and a conscientious label-reading partner? We live in a "take no prisoners" profit-motivated food jungle. We must be aware of carnivorous food-marketing predators out there. I'm not suggesting that we eat roots and berries although we'd probably be better off if we did. What can those of us who aren't that smart about eating do?

There's a quip (there's that word again) that says, "If it tastes good, spit it out." There's more truth in that than many of us want to admit. Do you know why? It's because of the free market system we live with. We choose to eat what tastes good. As stuffed as we get fast-food producers are up nights creating titillating treats to stuff us even more. Advertising agencies promote newer, larger, better, two-for-the-price-of-one goodies in a manner making it un-American not to eat them.

In the final analysis who decides what you and I eat? You and I do, that's who. We must pay attention, recognize and admit that WE are our biggest problem.

Suppose you pump more gasoline into your car than the car can consume? Suppose too that the fuel tank is expandable, that it will get bigger as you pump in more fuel. You either have to drive a whoooole lot more miles or get big as a house. It takes a lot of driving to get rid of a single "gallon" of gasoline. A better idea is not to put so much gasoline in the tank. Visit the gasoline station as often as you like just don't buy as much gasoline. Take your time. "Consume" it more slowly. Take smaller bites. Chew each bite longer. Take time to enjoy your meal.

I was talking to a doctor at the Mayo Clinic one time concerning weight and diets and such. Now the Mayo Clinic is way up there on the scale of authority. That doctor told me that, as far as losing weight was concerned, almost all diets will work. But what do you do after you've lost the weight? You either change eating habits to hold the weight down or the weight goes right back up again. He recommended not dieting just changing your eating habits. It works.

If you talk to someone who's been involved in survival training, ask them about eating. They'll tell you a person quickly reaches the point where they enjoy roots and berries – and bugs - and looks forward to the next opportunity to get them.

So, in the end, you're going to eat whatever, whenever, however you want to. This discussion is saying eat whatever you want just don't eat as much. Leave the table a bit hungry. If you want dessert, wait an hour. Your "fuel gauge" takes that long to register "full." You can do this! Be honest with yourself. You don't need any "easy as falling off a log" diet plan. Do it yourself. As Charlie Brown says, "We have met the enemy and he is us."

CR

Are you your own worst enemy?

My Friend

Let me tell you about this friend of mine. Actually he has his life and I have mine but we do interact along the way. He's a pretty good old boy actually. I don't tell him that because, well, because guys don't tell other guys things like that.

I found out something a day or so ago. Let me bounce it off of you and see what you make of it. The guy talks to machines. I don't mean like the comments you might make when your car gets stuck in the mud and you're late for an appointment and it seems that the very gods are conspiring against you. You might say "Darn!" or some other more colorful comment. Your automobile, of course, remains totally impassive. No, this fella talks to a machine, reasonably and logically in everyday conversational tones.

Are we getting close to a rubber room here? Do you think I should call on professional help? Let's "soldier on" a bit, gather a few more facts and see what you might conclude.

The guy I'm talking about is a graduate of the University of Michigan, an engineer of some sort. He quit that engineering thing some time ago but he can still talk, you know, "$E=MC^2$," formulas like that, and "algorithms." Algorithms! You know. That reasoning logic that says "If this, then that, and if not this, then something else." It's the language of Albert Einstein, guys like that.

Oh! And did I mention that he lives all alone too? He's not married. He's one of those people who spends too much of their time sitting in a bleak and empty apartment all by themselves with no one to talk to. I could tell you stories of old lumberjacks who'd been living like that, up in the bush, all by themselves over the winter. One of those old boys was having trouble with mice in the cabin. Mice are everywhere and are very prolific. I'm surprised the astronauts didn't run across mice on the moon. This old logger was able to control the mouse population in his cabin though. He had a thirty-thirty deer rifle that he kept beside his bunk. When a mouse ventured out – BANG! – and that mouse didn't venture out again. He had to plug bullet holes in the cabin wall but he kept the mice under control.

So anyway this guy's not married. He's all by himself evenings. He's alone in a cold, cruel world. Something else I'd better add here; the old boy has a taste for wine, the fruit of the grape. Now I'm not saying he drinks too much or anything like that but, you know, when a fella starts drinking when he's all alone, knockin' back a few all by himself, well, nuff said. It reminds me of the lyrics to a blues song that dates all the way back to Al Jolson: "And when it's twelve o'clock, I climb the stairs, I never knock for nobody's there. Just me and my shadow all alone and feeling blue." It's a sad, sad thing.

I've gotta add something else here. Not only does he talk to this machine but he tells me the machine talks back to him, yessir, tells him what to do. And what's more he does it! He has never done any harm to anything or anybody, at least not as far as I know, but the machine tells him to do things and he does them. To hear him tell about it, that machine is pretty smart. The things the machine tells him to do, he does, and they works he says. Think about that. He's successful in carrying out the instructions, instructions given him by a device without a heart or a pulse or the breath of life. It's just an impassive voice. He has become so taken with the assistance offered him by this impersonal voice-machine he hears that, the last I heard, he had proposed marriage. He didn't say how the voice answered that question. Now I've been married a couple times myself but never to a machine! You know, come to think of it now, maybe a machine – no – better not go there.

So! After hearing this heart-wrenching revelation of the lonely life of my bachelor friend, what do you think? Should I encourage him to check in somewhere and have his marbles counted?

CR

Learn to laugh a lot –
Mostly at yourself.

Written in the Snow

When I left the house this morning I noticed a fresh light snow had fallen last night. It was only a half inch or so but it managed to soften the evidence left by my two grandsons shoveling the porch. By the steps leading down to the wood yard were the tracks of squirrels. Beside the tracks I could see where they had taken apart a pine cone. I say "they" but I don't really know if there were several squirrels or just one that was very busy. It was probably just one. The tracks were very distinct and I easily identified them. There was the elongated hand with short "fingers" for the hind foot and a more proportional hand for the front. The squirrel had obviously been up early and had had breakfast – if that's what squirrels call it? – on the porch step.

I paused for a moment, reminiscing. I have read outdoor magazines and would marvel at the amazing stories the writer's told. I envied those outdoorsmen and women who could look at a set of tracks and read them like a book. They would look at the track and tell you what kind of animal it was, how long ago it had been there, its probable weight and where it was going. They might even tell you what it had for lunch.

I don't mean to belittle these outdoor authorities but you really don't have to be "the sharpest tool in the shed" to make some of those calls. Begin from this premise: nobody really knows, everybody's guessing. That's what Isaac Newton did when that apple fell on his head and Albert Einstein and Christopher Columbus and President Bush and the fella who runs the corner grocery store. When they're right they may go on to fame and glory and when they're wrong, well, maybe they'll guess better next time. Mistakes are caused by a lack of experience. Experience is gained by making mistakes. Accept that fact and the pressure eases considerably. You just make the best guess you can.

Let's get back to the tracks in the snow. When you see an animal run across the yard, take the time to walk over and look at the tracks. Pay attention to the details, the imprint, the spacing. Here's an example. Dog's tracks can be found almost everywhere, big ones, small ones, all sizes. The pads show plainly as do the claws. Dogs seem to wander everywhere, rambling, investigating the smell here and there and then rushing off to catch up with their owner. A fox's track on the other hand will have a similar paw print, claws and all, but it will be much smaller, daintier and will probably be in a neat straight line. If you look closely you will see that the rear foot is placed almost exactly where the front foot had been. The spacing of an animal's tracks will give an indication to how big it was and if it was walking or running.

The more of these patterns you look at and catalogue in your mind the better you'll get at "reading" them. Next time you see tracks, even if you don't see the animal that made them, you'll be able to read the story of what seemed to have happened.

Those squirrels I spoke of are regular visitors, tenants you might call them at our house. One reason is that we keep a feeder pretty well filled with sunflower seed and regularly scatter peanuts on the porch. We have some of the fattest squirrels in the area.

We have chipmunks too but they hibernate over the winter. They'll spend the summer days collecting those sunflower seeds and peanuts, stuffing their cheek pouches 'til you think they might burst. They they'll run off to their burrow and store them. I've watched them do this. In their burrow they'll have a sleeping area, a storage/pantry/dining area and even a separate area they use as a, as a, well as a bathroom. How do I know this? I didn't see them do those things but I read about it from what I judged to be a reliable source. I did see that the chipmunks disappeared as soon as snow arrived.

As far as outdoor writers who seem able to glance at a track and relate the animal's whole life history, well, a lot of that has come from experience. Most animals of a given type all act the same. They could probably have told the story they did without ever seeing the track. But, in order to "sell" the story it goes down better if it smacks of skill and daring-do.

I have heard this said of fishermen, "They riseth early and disturbeth the whole household. Mighty are their preparations and they goeth forth filled with hope. When they returneth, the day is far spent, they smelleth of strong drink and the truth is no longer in them." Now I didn't say that about the persons who write the outdoor hunting articles but I've got to admit I wonder at times.

CR

"Play Ball!"

"The flowers appear on the earth; the time of the singing of birds is come, and the voice of the turtle is heard in our land;" "Batter Up! Play Ball!" The first quote is from the Song of Solomon. The second is from me.

I have a grandson, Levi Charlebois, who is seven years old. He plays baseball. Thanks to the good offices of Joe and Susan Maki of Gwinn there is a "Little League" that Levi is a part of. Let me tell you about a game I watched between the Gwinn "Hoover's Auto

Body" and the Chatham "Lions." The age of the players in this Machine-Pitch League is from 6 to 8 years old. We'll talk more about that later.

Little League Baseball is supervised by a six-person group, civic minded citizens to whom we all owe a vote of thanks, to the families of the players, to the volunteers who help keep up the fields and equipment and those citizens and businesses who support the effort. Twenty or thirty years from now those kids are going to be the nation. They're the ones who are going to be operating your nursing home so pay attention.

The "leagues" are divided into: "T-Ball" league, 4 to 7 year olds; "Machine-Pitch" league, 6 to 8 year olds; "Minor" league, 7 to 10 year olds; and "Major" league, 11 and 12 year olds. Both Major and Minor leagues are further divided to boys and girls teams.

The game I attended was held in the evening at the Forsyth Township Athletic Field. The teams are supported by donations from individuals and local sponsors such as the "Hoover's Auto Body" of Gwinn who also provided team T-shirts. I'd like to say these sponsors are an exclusive group made up of only a select few but that would be a lie – well, maybe only a half a lie. There are a "select few" but it's not an "exclusive" group. Get involved! I'll tell you how in a minute.

So the cry went out, "Play Ball!" Kids erupted from both sides of the field. "Jimmy, you're first up. Put on your batting helmet." "Jacky, you're playing first base

– no, Jacky, FIRST base, you know, on the other side of the field." I've gotta say, my hat's off to those parents who coach these kids. It takes patience and dedication and patience and extra time after work and patience and keeping track of equipment and schedules and each other and - did I mention patience? It's like herding cats.

Anyway, the game is on! A machine an adult feeds balls into does the pitching. A "fast ball" is probably clocked at something like twelve miles per hour.

Jimmy takes a mighty swing. "Good swing, Jimmy, but next time wait 'til the ball gets there." Jimmy's not daunted in the slightest. He squares his shoulders in a manner that would do Ted Williams proud. There's the wind-up (actually the machine is always winding up). Here comes the ball! He swings! Crack! The ball rolls out between the pitcher and the third baseman. The third baseman doesn't move. The pitcher looks around. The center fielder and the second baseman run into each other. The left fielder chases the ball all the way to the fence. He throws the ball in the general direction of the pitcher. It hits the ground and rolls to a stop. The third baseman runs out and picks it up and throws it to – no! – wait! He doesn't throw it anywhere. It's OK though because the runner has stopped at first base. The next batter steps up to the plate. The pitcher walks out, gets the ball from the third baseman and throws it to the man operating the pitching machine. We're ready to go again.

It was a good game. The score was, lessee, "Hoover's

Auto Body" got a bunch of runs. The "Lions" got a whole lot of runs too including one home run that was hit to the shortstop. Grandpa was the winner – and probably a whole lot of other moms and dads and grandparents too.

I leaned on the fence and comment loudly, "The trouble here is with the coaching staff." When the coach turned around he had a big grin on his face. So did I. So did everyone else who attended that game.

If you'd like to get in on this, with a team, with a sponsorship, to contribute a couple bucks or just for a free evening's entertainment, get involved. There must be something like this near you. If there isn't, start one. It'll be worth the effort.

CR

The Eternal Debt

Dennis "The Lipper" Lipp

He fell off of a ladder. He broke his neck. He died. He was my friend.

Actually he was more than a friend. He and I were

a team that operated an F-4 "Phantom" fighter-bomber during that Viet Nam mess. I don't know what he might have thought of me because, you know, guys don't talk about things like that. I thought a lot of him but, of course, I didn't tell him either because, well, you know. It seems appropriate though that on this Memorial Day maybe I should say a few words about him. His name was Dennis Lipp. We all called him "The Lipper." I can speak more openly now because, well, he fell off a ladder and all this happened a long time ago.

There were people in Southeast Asia that were trying to kill Lipper and me back in those days. It was OK though because we were trying to mess them up a bit too. Things like that are permitted, in fact encouraged in a war, you know.

There were more than a few times when the grim reaper might have taken a slice of me – maybe both of us - if it hadn't been for the Lipper. On one mission we flew we helped pull a couple guys on a road watch team out of Laos. That was back when we were telling everybody we didn't have anybody in Laos. Lying is another of those things that seems to be permitted, even encouraged during a war. In fact, the first casualty of any war is the truth.

It was on that flight that Lipper re-jiggered our flight plan, re-computed our fuel requirement and found an alternate friendly field on which we could land. We threw "the book" out the window that day, Lipper and I. The calm cool action and superior job knowledge of the Lipper resulted in getting a couple guys out who wouldn't have made it otherwise. Our gamble paid off. Maybe I can tell you that story some other time. Anyway the powers that be were impressed enough to award us a couple medals. Unfortunately those medals disappeared somewhere in the great paperwork war. You folks out there who are GI or ex-GI know about things like that.

There's a bonding that happens between people who've been involved in life-or-death situations, who have to rely on one another. In those conditions who was "right" or who was "wrong" kind of fades away. Right and wrong judgments are more in the political spectrum and take place in more peaceful and secure areas after the smoke has cleared. In the thick of a battle a GI salutes and carries out the orders. Without that discipline and dedication there would be chaos and anarchy. There seems to be some of that in the Middle East right now. Iraq has the foreboding look of the Viet Nam thing all over again. Politics and religion seem to – well, I'd better not go there.

I would like to urge that you and I, at least on Memorial Day, put aside politics and religion and any other distractions. Focus on those GIs, past and present, the men and women who have always been there to answer the call. They simply salute and carried out the orders.

Another symbolic thing that carries special significance for the soldier: the American flag. That flag represents home and family. It's always been there with them wherever they might be. To you and me sitting comfortably at home or on a folding chair watching the parade pass by that flag may just be a part of the show. On this Memorial Day see it through the eyes of that legion of GIs who followed it, who took it forward with them wherever they went throughout the world. Never mind right or wrong, good or bad, they were there for you and me. They did it for us, for "we, the people" by the order of our elected representatives.

Next time the flag goes by, stand up. Never mind what the person next to you does or doesn't do. A salute or a hand over the heart would be even more appropriate. You won't be doing this for yourself or for me but for all those who are no longer able to be here. Do it because of what they did for you and for me. If, as you show your respect, no particular individual's name comes to mind, as a favor to me, think of "The Lipper."

Culinary Creativity

I get loose in Dorothy's kitchen now and again.
Dorothy tends to sit up late at night and sleep in morn-

ings. I, on the other hand, tend to hit the sack early, make several trips to the little boy's room during the night (that comes with age don't you know) and rise fairly early in the morning. The result is that I often fix my own breakfast.

"Captain Crunchies Cocoa Flakes" and "Handy-dandy-fruity-hooties" only hold their attraction for me - maybe twice. The second time only to see if they were really as bad as I remembered. I have grown fond of mixing and matching. I'll pour a little out of this box and a little out of that box and maybe a dash of something I find in Dorothy's spice drawer – usually something whose name I cannot pronounce much less understand what Dorothy uses it for. Lemme tell you, I can come up with concoctions that would make Doctor Frankenstein proud.

You remember Doctor Frankenstein, don't you? The fella whose assistant was Igor? "It's Alive! It's Alive!" Remember? He used to "dig things up" and put them together to make new things too. I guess all we creative persons tend to run along the same tracks.

Back to the kitchen. I have a fondness for pancakes, especially with blueberries. Dorothy gets me pancake mix "with blueberries." I want to tell you that one small pail of blueberries must keep that pancake mix plant running for days. Those blueberries are like the "pork" in a can of pork and beans. But am I discouraged? Does it dampen my spirits? Not at all! "Come, Igor, we must find our own fixens."

I have chopped up a quarter of an apple and added to the pancake mix – not half bad. I tried strawberries too but they lose something in the frying. A little dash of cinnamon can be a good thing but bananas are a definite no-no.

The grandkids come over for a visit now and then. Whenever they come for an over-night grandpa will try to talk them into a "special" breakfast. They seem to enjoy my flipping the pancake, frying pan and all, but when I lay out my culinary masterpiece before them you can tell from the expression on their faces that they are not exactly enthralled. "It's burned!" they say. "No, no," I explain, "that's just 'well done'." They aren't buying it though. Grandpa winds up eating the "well-done" pancake while the kids go back the "Crunchy-Wunchies."

Things seem to taste better when a person has created it himself. The fast-food business has destroyed much of the kitchen creativity of the past. Now when I speak of the past, I'm talking about a longer time ago than most of you remember. I don't remember there being any faster foods then than maybe a hamburger at a local restaurant. And, as I recall, that wasn't delivered all that fast either. We took more time to eat it back then too and it wasn't as big as they are now. There were times at home when mom would serve up a hot and tasty dish with a strange and unique name. I would find out in later life it was what she called leftovers. Mom was good. As modern marketers will tell you, "Sell the sizzle, not the steak!"

Here's another secret of the culinary masters that is lost in today's overweight society. In any dish you prepare, the tastiest ingredient is hunger. While in the service I remember having a grizzled old sergeant at a survival school instructing us in how to eat termites. Termites! Can't I just see some of you salivating out there? We had been in the mountains northwest of Reno, Nevada "living off the land" for just over a week. After that long without "home cookin" or any kind of cooking we were all listening pretty closely. The closest thing to "cooking" was when I had caught a couple of little brook trout and roasted them on a stick over an open fire. We ate them, bones and all. Anyway, for those of you who might be interested, when you eat a termite, when you get it in your mouth, you'd better bite fast or the termite will eat you. Beauty is in the eye of the beholder – and the hungrier you get, the more beautiful that termite looks.

Before closing I think I had better express my gratitude to my wife, Dorothy, and my step-daughter, Mary, who is a dietician. Their oversight and tactful suggestions have probably kept me from poisoning myself. The grandkids seem capable of watching out for themselves though. Say! Do you think my breakfasts might have something to do why Mary doesn't let the kids stay over more often?

CR

The Check-Out

My friend – I think he's still my friend? - had bought a new car. He and I make the rounds selling books at art shows and such and we usually go in his car. His car, the one he previously had, was a good one but, with all the books and the tables and the chairs and such, it was getting a little crowded. He bought a new car, a bigger one.

On our first trip in the new machine we went to the Curtis "Art on the Lake" show. He even made me wipe my feet before I got in the car. Then he backed 'er out onto the highway, switched gears – automatically, of course – and we were on our way, kings of the road! He nonchalantly moved the various levers and switches on the steering wheel and we just floated along. Suddenly, expressing alarm, he asked, "What's that target thing on the instrument panel? It just came on." I leaned over and looked. I saw what he was referring to. The thing was new to me. It was obviously new to him too.

"Maybe we should look in the owner's manual and see what it says," I offered. "Where's the owners' manual?"

He motioned toward the glove compartment – I guess they still call it that – which was pretty well concealed under the dash board. I hope you folks can follow what I'm talking about as I'm not up on modern automotive terminology. I found the owners' manual. It was encased in a leather zipper-cover thing kind of like the old family edition of the King James Bible. That doggone manual had more pages than most of the books we were selling.

Fumbling through it I finally found the pages – more than one page - that explained instrument panel symbols. I searched for the one we had seen. The pages were triple-columns of signs and symbols! "Here it is! Here it is! It says," I squinted at the fine print, "the cruise control is engaged." I looked up. "You got cruise control?"

He nodded very matter of factly. "It's got satellite radio too if I can figure out how to work it."

I looked closer at the "pilot's" seat in this new machine. The steering wheel alone had fifteen or twenty buttons and switches positioned up and down and across each side. I guess one of those buttons must be the horn but neither of us knew which it was. Now I've flown jet aircraft while in the Air Force and none of the cockpits in those aircraft were as complex as this machine seemed to be.

Suddenly the entire windshield went solid white! We couldn't see a thing. Knuckles on the steering wheel turned white also. The car weaved a little while we both frantically searched for a defogger and/or windshield wipers. Both of us were hoping and praying there was no one else on the road. One of us must have found the right switch, button or lever because two windshield wiper blades as long as your arm came up from wherever they were hidden. The fog was wiped off the outside of the windshield. We could see again, well, partially. There was still some fog on the inside.

"Where's the defroster?"

"It must be one of those buttons over there."

I pushed buttons and looked for levers. There were no levers. Suddenly cold air gushed from large ventilation holes in the dashboard. One of us must have done something right because the windshield began to clear. I was getting a little concerned. "Didn't the guy who sold you this thing show you how it works?"

"Yeah. We went for a drive."

I speculated that the salesmen's instructions must have stopped about the time he had the check for the purchase price in hand. Maybe, as long as the windshield fogs up now and then, the car should also have that "global positioning system" thing to tell a person where they were and how to get where they wanted to go. I don't know what else I might have said; maybe an off-hand remark or two about seeing-eye dogs and senior citizen assistance programs to teach how these new cars work. It was then I noticed my "pilot" was seriously studying the switches and levers on the steering wheel. "What are you lookin' for," I asked?

"I haven't found it yet but I think there's a 'passenger eject' button here somewhere."

We finished the trip in silence.

❧

It is the weak who are cruel.
Gentleness is to be expected
only from the strong.

"Why yes, I fly the jets!"

That was a popular line back in the early '50s when jet aircraft were still a sort of "new" thing. "Why, yes, I fly the jets." I was a pilot, a young bachelor in those days, stationed just north of Dallas, Texas. The Texas ladies, when they discovered a person was in the Air Force, would ask, "Do you fly the jets?" You would casually toss your silk scarf over your shoulder (figuratively that is) and reply, "Why, yes, I fly the jets." Immediately you were a somebody, you were IN! Those were the days. Some of you – mostly men - have asked why I don't write something about flying. Well, here's a story about flying:

This happened while I was an Aircraft Commander,

the pilot of a B-47 "Strato-jet" six engine jet bomber, a member of the United States Air Force's Strategic Air Command. We were "holding back the Russian Bear" by threatening Mr. Kruschev with nuclear annihilation if he got out of line. Boy! I'm certainly glad we never had to execute that threat. There would have been nuclear destruction and radiation everywhere. To stay sharp in our ability to do this we flew regular training missions, meeting take off times within +/-:03 minutes, refueling, navigating over long distances using celestial navigation. Celestial Navigation, You know, looking at the stars through a sextant, measuring the – ah, well - maybe we can talk about that another time.

We were flying the navigation segment of a mission this day. Navigation legs were pretty boring for the pilot and co-pilot. The co-pilot may get involved with taking a celestial observation for the navigator occasionally otherwise we just watched the engine instruments and monitored the auto pilot.

Sometimes, depending on the individuals involved, we'd play jokes on one another. On one flight we were at thirty some thousand feet (7 miles up in the air) flying a navigation leg. The aircraft was pressurized down to an altitude of about 8,000 feet. The navigator was at his position up in the nose of the aircraft doing the things that navigators do. The co-pilot and I were just trying to stay awake. I reached down and pulled the depressurization handle. Immediately cabin pressure shot up to thirty some thousand feet. The sudden expansion caused the air to cool and dense fog formed throughout the cockpit. That also happens when a person ejects, bails out.

The navigator was immediately on the intercom, his voice a couple octaves above normal, asking what had happened. When he heard the copilot and me giggling he knew what we had done. We reset the handle, repressurized the aircraft, and the navigator went back to navigating.

A little later the navigator was taking a break to eat his in-flight lunch. The flight lunch included a half-pint container of milk. He opened the milk carton completely, held it up to his sextant port, an opening to outside just in front of the pilot's windscreen, and opened the port. The cabin pressure immediately forced the milk to erupt through the sextant port like a volcano. My windshield suddenly went pure white! I couldn't see a thing. I grabbed the controls, checked the instruments and tried to figure out what had happened. Then I heard the navigator giggling.

The temperature up that high is about forty below zero. That milk froze immediately upon hitting the windshield. We flew the rest of the mission with a "white-out" windshield.

Arriving back at Lockbourne Air Force Base, we made a standard jet let-down for landing. The milk on the windshield did not melt and run off – it sublimated. The frozen milk turned from ice to vapor, leaving the white covering on the windshield. I couldn't see forward to land. What could we do? The navigator tried to splash water out the sextant port but, without pressure in the aircraft, it wasn't working.

While we were wondering what to do the co-pilot called approach control, a civilian radar control agency at Port Columbus Airport. "Do you have any rain showers in the area," he asked? "Why, yes, numerous rain showers," the controller replied. "Could you vector us through a rain shower please?" "Roger. Take up a heading of zero-nine-zero degrees for 13 miles." We did.

After a bit of silence, the controller, his curiosity obviously getting the better of him, asked, "Uh, why did you want to fly through a rain shower?" The co-pilot responded, "We want to wash the milk off of the windshield." This was followed by another period of silence. Then the controller once more keyed his microphone and asked, "Aah, Air Force Jet XXX, how did you get milk on your windshield?" Not missing a beat, the co-pilot responded, "We hit a cow." That was the end of the conversation. The rain shower subsequently cleared the windshield and we landed without further trouble.

I've often wondered though what that approach controller thought of all that?

CR

Cleaning Day

It's Sunday morning. I stretch luxuriously before getting up. Turning my head I look out the sliding glass door of our bedroom. The early light of dawn exposes a clear sky and the promise of a beautiful day. The door is open slightly and a soft breeze wafts into the room. At my side Dorothy breathes softly and regularly. She is inclined to sit up late watching baseball games and knitting and crocheting and things that women do. I, on the other hand, am inclined to retire early and get up early to enjoy the quiet splendor as the day arrives. I slip out of bed closing the bedroom door quietly behind me. Life is good.

I have a little exercise routine I do every morning, a reduced routine on weekends, and then relax and watch the sun come up, coffee in hand. The geese set up a cackle outside on the bayou. I feed them every morning and they're getting impatient. The ducks are there too and the seagulls and the squirrels and the chipmunks and goldfinches and a whole menagerie. A family of fox, momma and five kits, have taken up residence under the floor of the old log cabin next door. Its fun watching them roll and tumble and play with one another. Then momma comes home with a mouse she's caught out in the marsh and the little ones go wild. Yeah, life is good.

I hear sounds from back toward the bedroom. Dorothy must be getting up. I've already looked over the Sunday Paper and laid it on the kitchen table where Dorothy will find it – but she doesn't come out. The noises continue in the other end of the house and I wonder why she hasn't come out to say "Good Morning" or something? Cup in hand I wander back toward the bedroom. Turning the corner into the hallway I am suddenly filled with apprehension. Mops and pails and brushes and dusting "things" surround the vacuum cleaner. I resolutely brace myself to meeting Dorothy in "house cleaning mode." Then do what wise husbands have been doing ever since Adam when Eve cleaned those apples out of the Garden of Eden. I flee.

Grabbing up my laptop computer and a CD to watch, I head for cover at the Beach House. Fortunately I have pre-positioned supplies out there, coffee, cookies, the essentials. Twenty years in the military have taught me the need for considering logistics – be prepared! Now before some of you ladies come down on me for not offering to help with the house cleaning, know that I have "been there – done that." Experience has taught me the best thing I can do is clear the area; Weapons of Mass Destruction are soon to be released against dust, dirt and all things that clutter the area. That would seem to include me. Best I go far enough to be clear of the "collateral damage" area.

I do get a little ambition while I'm at the beach house. Call it a guilty conscience. The floor tends to get pretty sandy. Well, what do you expect? The place is on the beach. I shuffle the meager furniture around, pick up the carpets, shake them outside and sweep the floor. Having completed that task, the equivalent of Hercules and the Aegean stables, I have to admit the place looks considerably neater. I am able to successfully fight off the urge to do anything more. With the clean up efforts

I have worked up a sweat. No wonder! The thermometer outside reads 80 degrees – and it's in the shade. I've noticed a couple fishermen slowly trolling back and forth in the lake in front of the cabin. A sailboat a little farther off shore leans with the freshening wind. A fancy looking powerboat cruises by with a water skier trailing behind.

You know, I've got a bathing suit stashed out here somewhere. Be prepared, remember? I'm soon in my bathing suit and headed toward the water. I pause beside some charred sticks remembering the "campfire" grandson Levi and I shared here a couple days ago. Yeah, life is good. Then I dip my toe into Lake Superior. Yeeeow! That cold water is incentive for that water skier not to be trying anything fancy and risk falling in! Maybe this swimming thing wasn't such a good idea? But how am I gonna tell Levi that grandpa started out for a swim, tested the water, and ran back inside the beach house? Gathering all my courage and putting common sense aside I stride purposefully out into deeper water. Ha! It's not as bad as I first thought. My feet and the calves of my legs quickly lose all sense of feeling in that ice water. About thigh deep I take a deep breath and plunge in like a great big ole whale – and shoot back out in a manner that would put a penguin to shame. Wow! There's slush in my kidneys! Back to the beach and it didn't take me long to get there. The sun quickly returns feeling to my extremities and I'm able to get back to the beach house.

Cleaning Day

Hey! There's a football game on the television. It's only a little nine-inch TV screen and receives two, maybe three channels on a good day if you squint. I don't usually come out here to watch TV. I wonder if that war back at the main house has been won yet? Dare I go look? I think I'll watch the ball game awhile instead.

03

A brave man knows when to take cover.

CR

Count Your Blessings

The headlines have moved on to other subjects. The evening news says there was an election in Iraq. Our President is explaining himself yet again before the TV cameras. The price of gasoline came down – and then went up again. The World Trade Organization is adjusting or readjusting tariffs – or whatever it is that World Trade Organizations do. If you ask about Katrina the answer you're apt to get might be "Isn't she that new girl down at the . . .?" No, the Katrina is that "girl" who came ashore down on the Gulf of Mexico. She filled our TV screens for days with images of wailing people stranded on a bridge, bursting levees, disorganized officials pointing accusatory fingers at each other. All officialdom seemed to be wailing that the sky was falling, - and it was somebody else's fault. Every now and again there'd be a glimpse of a National Guardsman or woman trying to maintain order. Coast Guard helicopters or people in rowboats would be rescuing folks stranded on rooftops.

Finally the water level went down – and so did the major news stories. It all moved on to other things. While all this was going on the Federal Emergency Management Agency (FEMA) was rushing around bumping into itself while trying to figure out what it should do. Folks on the Gulf Coast were left to look at the wreckage of what had once been their homes. Do you think all this might have something to do with that first amendment separation of Church and State?

Well, there doesn't seem to be much publicity connected with what I'm going to tell you next but I believe it's something that can make you and me and everybody else proud to be counted as Americans. The particular group I refer to in this example is from Big Bay's Presbyterian Church but there are groups from other churches, denominations involved. There are even a few heathens that think that way, folks who pitched in to help.

The Big Bay group was duly assigned a time and place: the 19th through the 26th of November at Gautier, Mississippi – right on the Gulf Coast. They would spend Thanksgiving in a tent city with outdoor "facilities." The pastor's wife wrestled pots and pans cooking meals to feed them. Individual crews were assigned to "de-mould" some of the 5,000 homes that had been inundated by the 8 foot deep flood waters. Dry-wall and insulation had been removed by a previous crew. The next job was scraping and scrubbing walls, treating them with bleach to stop the mold growth and then scrubbing them down yet again. These were not photo-opportunities for newsreel cameras but "scut" work that had to be done. Where did the money come from for travel and living expenses? Most of it came out of the pockets of the volunteers.

The pastor and his wife left their home in Upper Michigan with a car and trailer packed with supplies at

8:00 AM on a Friday morning. The supplies had been purchased locally from GFS foods which gave them a discount on groceries. The Coca Cola folks donated several cases of fresh drinking water – a necessity in the vast polluted area into which they were going. Cram's General Store in Big Bay sent them on there way with a full tank of gasoline. The Payne's made the 1,350 mile trip in two days. They spent that Friday night "snoozing" in their car in a rest area arriving at Gautiere, Louisiana, on Saturday evening.

Volunteers all wore identification tags and a distinct blue and white "T" shirt for security reasons. Local folks needed to be able to identify volunteers from strangers, possible looters, in their community. Jerry Lee's Grocery in Gautiere gave them generous discounts. One day, while the parson's wife was buying groceries, a local resident recognized her as a volunteer. The woman rushed up, gave her a big hug and thanked her for coming down to help. Something to do with Thanksgiving, wouldn't you say? All this supports a theory of mine: The best sermons are not preached from pulpits,

After returning home Lauri Tallio, a local school teacher, created a thirty minute documentary of their trip. She volunteered to show it and speak about the experience to any groups who might be interested. Plans are already under way for the next trip. It is estimated the Gulf area recovery effort, much like the Iraq war, will be an ongoing thing - for five or more years.

The rest of us can feel particularly blessed at this

time of year and it's a good time to remember our neighbors. From contributions as little as "the widow's mite"
through sacrifices as great as the crucifixion, each one
of us should be able to find some way to help. Next time
you get to thinking "people are just no d--n good," think
of those volunteers.

ॐ

"It's Not Your Fault!"

"Do you have trouble staying on a diet because you're always hungry? It's not your fault!"

That was the opening line on a TV ad. That's a heck of a good opener, isn't it? So many of us are overweight and we all want to lose "a few pounds." (Fill in the "few pounds" yourself.) The money we spend on diet plans and pills and potions and programs to lose weight "effortlessly" would pay the dollar and cents cost of the Iraqi War.

We all know how hard it is to lose weight. How gloriously comforting is that sweet sounding statement: It's not your fault. You are in love with the adman who said that. The ad goes on to describe a miraculous plan that will do everything for you painlessly and without effort. No complicated diet. No giving up the foods you crave. No hunger pangs. No sweat. Nothing! After all, "it's not your fault." Do you believe all that? The only thing that'll do all that "effortlessly" is death.

But back to the advertisement: The ad first grabs your attention with, "trouble staying on a diet." It's saying here's a soft shoulder to cry on, "it's not your fault." You're immediately ready to follow that sympathetic voice anywhere. And here's where it leads: "For only "X" payments of "Y" dollars etc. etc. whatever"

They're offering an exercise machines that will help you exercise "effortlessly." I'm waiting for the next advance, a machine with an electric motor that can be programmed to perform your exercises automatically. You won't even have to be there. Won't that be "effort-less?" The guy or gal who invents that machine will be having lunch with Bill Gates in no time.

Do you really believe all that high-priced Madison Avenue advertising? We want to believe – but it ain't necessarily so! These are the same hucksters who have us eating "Mammoth Burgers" with a "super-sized" order of 'fries.

Why do we believe all that advertising? We believe it because we WANT to believe it! We yearn to lose weight in a way that's as easy as munching that burger and fries. It's not going to happen.

But "it's not your fault," remember? That was the hook. Well, if it's not your fault, then whose fault is it?

Dear heart, this may be where you want to stop reading. I've got an answer – it worked for me – but you may not like it. Hold your nose! Here's the medicine: If "it's not your fault," whose fault is it? In your heart, you already know the answer. You can talk about "glands" and "big-bones" and "inherited genes" but those are pacifiers. It IS what you EAT that pushes up the weight isn't it? It's you that feeds you. You transport that burger and fries to your mouth.

There are folks who can eat more and still weigh

less. Some of us can't: accept that. The only consolation
is, if there's ever a famine, they'll be the one's who'll
probably starve first.

I once flew airplanes for General Curtis Lemay
in the Strategic Air Command. He didn't cut slack for
anyone. There was no "it's not your fault." A comment
once attributed to him was, "I have neither the time nor
the inclination to differentiate between the incompetent
and the unfortunate!" The folks he was talking to got
fired! He demanded results! He got results! And, believe
me, they weren't easy to attain but I learned that if you
grit your teeth and just do it, it can be done.

Here are a few suggestions that'll help: Don't buy
things that you shouldn't eat, things that have lots of fat
and calories, things that "taste good." If you don't buy
it, you won't eat it. Secondly, lose that opiate Madison
Avenue vision that you won't be hungry. You've got a
large "food warehouse" down there and it's going to beg
and plead and wheedle and cry. Grit your teeth! You've
just got to say "NO!" You're going to be hungry – all
the time. Accept it! Analyze your craving for food. Is it
just "mouth hunger," a craving for "taste?"

Find something to do, something that you enjoy
then do it in intensely. It'll help take your mind off of
eating. As years go by those hunger pangs will decrease
but they'll still be there. You're going to have to learn
to live with them – believe me.

Join a "weight-watcher" group of some kind where

folks can support one another. Set goals and log your weight progress where everyone can see it. That visual display provides added incentive. Your weight will go down - and back up - and down again. Grit your teeth! Keep at it.

Exercise too. Exercise is good! It's necessary! If you'll exercise for a month or two you'll notice how much better you feel. As far exercising to lose weight though, do you know how much exercise that'll take? Think of Albert Einstein's formula, $E=MC2$: "E" (Exercise) equals "M" (Mass you want to lose in pounds) times "C" (the speed of light, 186,000 miles per second) squared. That's a whoooole lot of exercising.

As hard as not-eating is, it's the only thing that'll work. This over-weight thing is – well - whose fault is it anyway? (Please! Don't think to "kill the messenger.")

CR

Efficiency!

This season of year our land is decked out in multicolored magnificence. With time-conscious intensity our daily lives are devoured by what we aptly call the rat race. We all too often sacrificed quality in the name of efficiency. We have become so goal oriented in our drive to see the forest that we have cut down the trees.

All you Daniel (and Danielle) Boones out there are eager to go hunting. You can't get but a couple days off – maybe just a weekend. You get 'hold of the fellas, call ahead to get things ready. A blind is set up. A bait pile a hundred fifty feet or so down a clear alley from the blind is arranged. It's been tended regularly for the past couple weeks. Several deer have gotten in the habit of visiting the bait pile regularly. One of them has a beautiful six-point rack. Great!

You recheck your schedule. You can make it up there, lessee, Friday night but you'll be getting in late. That's OK. Sunup is getting later and later these days anyway and you'll be able to drive almost up to the blind. There's no electricity out there. It's still a bit primitive but you'll be able to have a "continental breakfast" and hot coffee from a propane stove. It won't be so bad. That big buck has been coming in pretty regularly just at daybreak and that six point rack will make it all worthwhile.

Just after sunup that first day, right over your second cup of coffee that six pointer shows up. You're able to knock it down with one shot. With the help of the other guys you're able to gut it, drag it out and get back to the Thunder Bay Inn in time for a hot lunch. One of the guys knows a taxidermist who'll mount the head for you. The carcass, well, we'll give it to the "poor and needy." That little gesture kind of gives you a warm altruistic feeling. You find you can grab a nap this afternoon and still be up in time to swap stories at the bar Saturday night. Sleep in late Sunday and be right back at the job early Monday morning. There's nothing like a successful deer hunt to give a person that feeling of making contact with their roots. You'll have to admit that was efficient – if your goal was simply to kill a deer.

Real life – I mean the way things still are for many of us – probably is not that "efficient." We go out to enjoy the camaraderie of a deer hunting camp, where guys – or gals – will gather, pull a cork or two and regale one another with tales of past daring do. The range of our shots gets longer. The racks on the deer get bigger. Hunting conditions get worse. The deer gets cleverer but, of course, we are cleverer still. And the eatin' out at the camp, the meals are great. But what ever happened to the hunt? Well hunting, old fashioned hunting that is, just isn't efficient.

Have you heard? Enterprising operators are setting up hunting preserves now. They're kinda like cattle ranches but for deer, you know? Kinda like that Elk hunt they have downstate. What with the big lumber and paper companies selling off their commercial forest reserve land and all the apple knockers from down state buying forties here and there, gating the roads and posting the land, it won't be long before there'll be nowhere to hunt anyway. You won't be able to go looking for the deer. You'll have to get the deer to come to you, hence the bait pile.

Maybe that's so. I haven't hunted with anything but a camera for the past – oh – a good many years now. My last time out with a rifle I was sitting at a lunch spot I had under a hemlock tree. It was on a ridge at the foot of a big rock outcrop. I was just sitting there, knees raised, holding the rifle between my knees. I glanced up and suddenly there, just a couple hundred feet away, came this little buck.

This was his area. He knew this area like the back of his – well – like the back of his hoof and he was wary. He didn't seem to remember that lump of whatever he was seeing at the base of that hemlock tree. I didn't move – not even my eyes. He came a little closer. He looked at me hard. He moved his head to one side, then the other. I didn't move. He came closer yet, maybe thirty feet away, and stopped again. I hadn't moved. He stamped his foot and snorted. I didn't move. We looked at one another for maybe a minute and a half. Finally he tossed his head and evidently accepted whatever that was under the tree. He wandered down a draw pausing to scratch for and munch on fallen acorns now and then. I just sat there watching him. After he had wandered away, I looked at the rifle in my hands and asked myself, "Why are you toting this thing around?"

Don't misunderstand. I'm not a vegetarian. If you were roasting up some venison I wouldn't turn down an invitation. I guess I just enjoy the hunt more than the kill. But then again I'm going to be 78 years old the first day of this deer hunting season. I guess I'm just not that efficient anymore.

CR

First Time Fishin'

Fish

"Can we go fishin', grandpa?"

My five-year-old grandson, Levi Charlebois, and I had been out to the beach in front of our house. We had tested the water – several times – explored, picked up sticks and threw them in the lake and played tag, which wore grandpa out completely. Then he dug a hole in the sand for us to start a small fire. This had become a sort of custom for us to have a small "campfire." I watch him playing in the sand and we talked. We do things together and I think he may be picking up some of his grandpa's likes and dislikes. We even talk about God now and then – just a little bit, mostly him telling me what he has heard from his little friends. I try to guide him a little but I believe the best "sermons" are lived, not preached. Maybe we can talk more seriously in that area when he gets a little older.

On the way back to the house we explore the marsh and stop to investigate the flowers and to test the muck to see how deep it is. Grandpa is hard pressed to answer all his questions and "I don't know" comes out frequently. Kids see and think and wonder and ask why about things we oldsters have just accepted somewhere along the line. That wonder is a good thing I only wish I knew more answers.

When we got to the dock in front of the house we stop to watch the geese and the ducks on the bayou and to watch for turtles. Right at out feet, in the water beside the dock, fish were swimming about feeding on the sandy bottom. That's when he looked up at me and asked "Can we go fishin', grandpa?"

"When do you want to go fishing?"

"Right now!"

I find it difficult to say "no" to that boy, a condition I hope his momma doesn't look into too closely. "OK. Let's go get a fishing pole and, lessee, maybe we can use some bread crusts for bait."

"Why don't we use worms?"

"Where'll we get the worms?"

"We can dig in the sand." That was followed by a discussion of the habits of worms and where they might and might not be. We decided we'd try the bread and, if that didn't work, we'd try something else.

It didn't take long to find a pole and a hook and get it all together.

"Aren't you gonna fish, grandpa?"

"I think, today, I'll just watch you."

I had flattened the barb on the little number 10 hook to make it easier to "catch and release" fish. Getting the bread to stay on that little hook was a bit of a trick. When we put it in the water any sudden movement would cause the bread to come off. An added benefit was the proximity of the fish, the clear water and the sandy bottom. We could watch the action and reaction of the fish, learn what their habits were, see how they approached and took the bait. We had a first rate fishing classroom right there in front of us. Levi quickly learned that his shadow in the water and sudden movements frightened the fish away. We laid the pole on the dock so unintentional movement, amplified by the length of the pole wouldn't "jiggle" the bait frightening the fish and/or causing the bread to come off the hook. Patience was another thing he was learning because as – whoa! You got one! The bobber skated across the surface as the fish moved away. Levi scrambled to grab the fish pole. Of course we could see this entire happening too in the clear water. The action of the rod with the fish tugging was, well you fishermen out there know the rush you get when you "got one" on the line.

Levi's whole face lit up, shining like the sun. He raised the pole. The fish came out of the water wiggling and wriggling and trying to get free. Levi raised the pole higher. The fish, of course, swung toward him. Levi was tried to dodge but the fish always swung toward the fishing pole he was holding. Grandpa was watching and having more fun than he'd had in a long time. I grabbed the line and ran my free hand down to get 'hold of the fish, a little six or eight-inch bullhead. We hollered for grandma and momma to come see the fish and, of course, take some pictures.

After the pictures had been taken and everyone had "ooohed" and "aaaahed" appropriately, we let the fish go. Grandpa rebaited the hook and we were at it again. I lost count of the number of fish he caught but he kept his grandpa busy taking them off of the hook and letting them go again. We were fortunate that the fish were there and biting. I feed them regularly 'most every day but they seem to have their own schedule and sometimes they're there and sometimes not.

When we finally tired of fishing Levi couldn't wait to get home and tell his daddy about goin' fishin'. I'm sure that next time he comes, first thing he's going to do is look up at grandpa – and grandpa can't say "no". You know, it's a special privilege to be able to take a youngster, boy or girl, on their first fishing expedition – especially when it's as successful as Levi's. Having done that, have I created a monster?

‿

"Democracy is the worst form of
government - except for all those
others that have been tried."
-Winston Churchill

Where Flamingo's Fly

"Have you seen what's out in front of your house?"

"What? What are you talkin' about?"

"Flamingos!"

"Flamingos? Have you been sniffin' glue again?"

My neighbor stepped aside and pointed. "Look!"

There, lining both sides of our driveway were a flock of Flamingos. Flamingos? In Upper Michigan? There must have been one heck of a windstorm down Florida way to blow Flamingos all the way to the wilds of Northern Michigan.

Now you know there's gotta be some kind of explanation for this. A flock of Flamingos doesn't just suddenly appear in a person's front yard. Upon closer examination we found a small sign post among the flock of Flamingos, a small notice stating, "You've been flocked!" There was also a telephone number to call to arrange to have the flock of flamingos "fly" elsewhere.

But the story's not over. Upon calling the designated number, the phone rang four or five times and a recording machine began singing "Happy Birthday to you, Happy Birthday to you." All of us have experienced the wonders and convenience of modern electronics and mechanization in our brave new world – the frustration of having a machine tell you, "your call is important to us etc. etc." It's maddening when you're unable to talk at all much less trying to communicate with something that doesn't even have a pulse. Oh, well, "happy birthday" is an improvement over "your call is important."

It turns out that the flamingo program is the brainchild of Brian Wibby and Heidi Mager. They are a part of the Better Future Program of Child and Family Services of the Marquette County Health Department. Specifically Brian and Heidi are with the Big Brothers and Sisters program of Marquette County. Considering all those bureaucratic titles I guess I should be happy that answering machine chose to sing "Happy Birthday."

Brian and Heidi "arrange" to have the Flamingos alight in your yard in the hope that you will contribute $10.00 to have them shooed away. (If you don't care to play the game, they'll remove the much-saddened birds after approximately 24 hours anyway.) On the other hand, if you should suddenly think of someone whose life might be brightened (or complicated?) by the sudden arrival of a flock of Flamingos on their front lawn why, for a contribution of $20.00 that, too, can be arranged – strictly on the "QT" of course. No one need ever know who sent what to whom or where or when or why. I think Brian and Heidi are affiliated with the Central Intelligence Agency somehow – or maybe with Sergeant Schultz from the old TV show, "Hogan's Heroes," remember? "I know nothing! Nothing!"

In spite of the "Happy Birthday" answering machine and the "further instructions located in the envelope on the rear of this sign" – which were not - the program is good and has been initiated to serve the needs of a good cause. Above all their hearts are in the right place. So what did I do? I waved my cane at them and shouted, "Bah! Humbug!" – and all the flamingoes flew away - to somebody else's yard.

Now this next is strictly in confidence and should remain solely between you and I. If you would like to get involved, you know, "flock" somebody, here's how you can do it: Call XXX or XXX at XXX-XXX, extension XXX. To maintain security call on your "shoe" telephone. The proper coded communication should begin, "Hello, Chief, this is Max. About those flamingos . . ."

CR

Live in such a way that, if someone
Says bad things about you,
No one will believe them.

Let us give Thanks

"The oil companies are gouging us for high profits!"
"Our city commission is acting like its Disney Land
north!" "My wife (husband) doesn't understand me!"
I'm sure you can add to this list with "pet peeves"
of your own ranging from the politicians leading our
country to the check out clerk at the corner store and
that sassy teenage kid who lives down the street. Am I
going to try to convince you these things aren't true? No
I'm not. But, if you look at these things from a different
angle they are the very characteristics that we should be
appreciating in our United States.

Consider the plight of an Iraqi citizens just a few
years ago. That Disneyland crack would pretty well assure they wouldn't be around to see the next sunrise. If
you think that's a unique situation, that there are no other
societies like that, look at some of those South African
countries, look at North Korea. Of course most of the
"blue collar" folks in North Korea are so involved in a
desperate struggle to find enough to eat that they have
neither the time nor the inclination to criticize anybody.
Their diets are so poor that children are becoming men-
tally impaired; their little brains are not able to develop
normally. And no one complains about "the glorious
leader" – not unless they have a death wish.

Maybe you feel that you can find a country – New Zealand for example or one of the Scandinavian countries – that you think might have a better medical system than we do. Consider also that they have a long waiting list for treatment unless you can afford better care and, if you are past a particular age (it varies depending on the malady) you are in the same position as an older car that's considered no longer cost effective to repair. I'm not saying that all our systems, methods, ways for doing whatever is the best that exists but I am saying it's up to you and me to change it. The opportunity, the machinery is there for us to affect these things but it's not easy to do it. Those of you who are thinking "Yeah, but . . ." have a point. On the other hand, quit your bitchin'. Get off your backside and get out there and do something. Henry Ford once said, "If you think you can – or if you think you can't, you're probably right." There's more truth than "just cute" to that comment.

There are so many opportunities, so many activities, and so much freedom available to each of us and yet we don't seem to realize it. The reason we as a people have achieved a leading role in the world is because of this freedom, because we release our people to strive to be as much as they can be. We often have disagreements over what should or shouldn't be done. Some are violent such as the Civil War, for example. Others involve whether or not to allow someone to use a cell phone while driving. The outcomes usually involve compromises that hopefully make the country, the society even stronger.

How wonderful it is. The opportunities are there if we just turn off the TV, get your butt off the couch and take advantage of them

I've often thought, if I were a politician and speaking at public gathering, here's what I'd do: when it was time for questions from the audience and someone asked me something I would first ask them if they had voted in the last election. I wouldn't ask which way or for whom they had voted, just if they had voted. If their answer involved some explanation involving "snow capped mountains or shark infested waters" – in other words why they hadn't exercised that right, I would simply nod and turn to the next questioner. When the person who asked a question HAD voted in the last election, I would discuss their question with them.

Yes, we do have problems in our country. Some of our politicians are crooks. Some of the check-out clerks are having identity problems and the kid down the street might not have had his butt paddled a time or two when it should have been. But we also have politicians who aren't in the business "just for the money," store clerks who are efficient and polite, and a kid next door who is courteous and helpful and won't take a nickel for it. We're just not as apt to notice them as we are the "bad apples" and that's our fault. Appreciate those people! Think more often about the honest politician, that courteous clerk, the helpful teenager and be thankful for them and you remember to say "please" and "thank you" when it's appropriate. There's an expression, "is the glass half full or half empty?" I'd go further than that. If you look, really look at it, the glass is a lot more than half full. We seem to be conditioned to measure the "empty." A special day is here each year for giving thanks. Think about that. We've got a whole lot to be thankful for.

❧

Gone Fishin'

Maybe all of you aren't familiar with some of the details of this next story but I have seen, and any farmer will tell you, that cows are creatures of habit. When it's time for the cows to come home, to come to the barn the farmer or herdsman doesn't have to mount his horse and ride off "on the range" to round them up. He'll just go out to the gate to the barn. The cows will all be there waiting for him. In fact, if he's a little late, the cows will delicately bellow to get him to pay attention to business. We've probably all seen pets or other animals doing things that make you wonder just how much thought, how much knowledge lies behind those big bland eyes. The woods are full of stories about pets that have awakened their masters and mistresses when the house had caught fire.

Of course that kind of instinctive reaction doesn't apply to us, to we humans, we, the most advanced of all God's creatures. We're not creatures enslaved by habit, are we?

The last Saturday in April is the opening day of trout fishing season. I have been out there in the pasture for a good number of years but when April rolls around there's an instinct to dig out the fishing pole and check the action of the reel, the availability of hooks, line and leader. The outdoor magazines are lying on the coffee table. Past fishing trips wander into and out of my memory. In my mind's eye the adventures grow along with the size of the fish caught. One aside observation here for the benefit of you workaholics out there: You won't have these memories to revert to in later years as you look deep into the fireplace unless you get out and capture them now. "The bird of time has but a little way to fly, and lo, the bird is already on the wing."

Back to the cows and I. I am indeed fortunate in that my mother built her home on a beautiful spot on the shore of Lake Superior. Now Dorothy and I live there. It's within walking distance of the mouth of the Chocolay River. It's the end of April. Fishing pole in hand, just like those cows, that "last Saturday" finds me at the mouth of the Chocolay River. Spring, at least this early, doesn't always arrange warm and comfortable days for that l ast Saturday but the true trout fisherman hardly notices. That day finds them bellowing at the gate and ready to wet a line.

Maybe it has something to do with the number of "last Saturdays in April" I have already seen but I don't go out there hysterically beating the water to a froth in a quest for fish. I listen to the flowing water gurgling around a couple of ancient pilings that have been there I guess since that Fella walked on the water that time. Buds on the trees and bushes are swelling with new life. Along the shore are bits and pieces of whatever has been drifting down the river since who knows when. And along the shore, close to the water where the sand is firm, the tracks I made getting here are relentlessly being obliterated, the relentless waters washing clean the sands of time. There's a pretty clear message there. Whenever you begin to feel self-important, poke your finger into the water, and then notice the hole it leaves when you take it out.

A breeze wafts out of the southwest. With a little imagination it's a gentle breeze. I get a line in the water, hook and bait a couple feet below a bobber, the pole propped against one of those old pilings, propped solid with a convenient rock. The water of the lake is smooth and deep blue and sparkling as the sun reflects off the wind raised ripples. The mouth of the river wavers and varies over days as the strength and currents of the river clash with the winds and the waves of the lake. It's always the same but ever different. The bobber is – is – where is that bobber? Oh, well, no matter. If anything of consequences takes the bait the pole tip will indicate it. With a little luck the fish may not bother me at all.

A seasoned fisherman will usually bring a sandwich along too. I like to start a small fire and toast the sandwich before eating it. If it gets a little burnt why that's OK too. Maybe it falls in the fire, gets a little ash on it. It's all part of the game and I love it.

I've got a couple little grandsons who live nearby. When they grow a little more I'll be bringing them down here to learn about the wind and the water and what's important in life.

CR

The Hunt

These next remarks may cost me half my readers. They'll both probably leave me and turn to the editorial page, but I just gotta say something.

I was born and raised on a small farm just outside Marquette. My father was a policeman so guns, although not prominently displayed at home, were not unfamiliar to me. So was hunting something I did? Is the grass green in spring? Sure I did. We also had a cabin in the woods up on the Yellow Dog River. A bunch of us would gather up there each autumn to take part in that ritual known as deer hunting. We'd tramp the beautiful fall forests returning to camp with tales about the adventures of the day, often embellished a little. We would throw dinner scraps out evenings and a deer or two might stop by for a meal. It wasn't a consistent thing as this was also their "season of amour" and – well – you know how that goes. Feeding them seemed the fair thing to do. We chased them through the bushes all day it seemed right to offer them a snack in the evening. This was supposed to be a sport although the deer might have had other thoughts about that. There was laughter and tall tales and good fellowship, camaraderie and memories that lasted for years.

I understand a lot of the guys who were in the military, those involved in the shooting part of a war, often had no urge to hunt when they came back. Not all of them but a number large enough to be significant. Maybe a little time spent as the "huntee" changed their view of hunting.

There have been changes to the hunting experience too. With ATVs and four-wheel drive vehicles and access roads to nearly everywhere deer camp, as it used to be, has become a thing of the past. There are more and more and more people in the world today and we're taking over the deer's habitat. Fortunately the deer have been able to adapt. They have learned to live very comfortably among us – too comfortable according to some of us. Other animals that have not been so adaptable have disappeared.

A lot of today's hunting involves a bait pile. That use to be illegal. Near this bait pile, within rifle or pistol or bow-and-arrow range, would be a hunting blind – also illegal in the old days. These hunting blinds can be very elaborate structures. They may be heated, include an easy chair and may even have a television set. That doesn't resemble the hunting experience of old. It just doesn't seem sporting to invite someone or something to dinner then shoot them as they sit down to eat. That's more like a contract for a mafia "hit man."

Another new change is the hunting reservation. So much of what used to be open woodland has been divided and subdivided, sold, fenced, gated and "no trespassing" signs everywhere. Less and less area is open for hunting, even the bait-and-shoot hunting. Enterprising entrepreneurs (did I spell that right?) have bought and enclosed large acreages, bred game animals thereon and created a hunting resort. There's a fee for a hunting that often includes a room or a cabin. That allows a person to hunt but there's an additional charge for whatever game is shot. The fee might be based upon weight or antlers or whatever criteria had been established. The evolving land situation seems to be creating this market.

Here's another development. I was reading a hunting story. The hunter "lined up the cross hairs just behind the shoulder, easy, eeeeasy, press the button on the mouse – and . . and it . . . ." Press the button on the mouse? Was this a video game? No, it wasn't! This hunter is sitting at home looking at a computer screen. He's remotely sighting an automated rifle located at a game farm many miles away. The rifle is fastened to another electronic gadget. And this was not an artificial target but a live animal. Once the "button" has been "pressed" and the animal has been shot arrangements can be made for dressing shipping and/or taxidermy but that's an extra expense. Some part of the hunting experience is missing here. This is like an Arnold Schwarzenegger movie or a violent interactive video game.

You know, I could serve you a slice of bologna and called it venison steak. But if you had ever eaten a venison steak you'd know that this is baloney. If you had never eaten venison though . . .?

CR

Independence – or Not?

Once more into the breech, dear friends, in celebration of our Declaration Of Independence. We presented that declaration to the British in particular (at the time) but also as a statement to the world in general. And if you look into the history surrounding that action we probably should have gotten our butts kicked except for several favorable breaks at the time. The British were preoccupied with problems elsewhere in the world of that day while the French saw a personal benefit to encouraging our continued harassment of the British. Ah, but as Napoleon Bonaparte once said, "History is a collection of lies that has been agreed upon" - and it's written by the winners. Whatever clouds and uncertainties blur the past, we must all agree that declaration move certainly has turned out well for all of us living here today. There are undoubtedly some among us who might argue that point but the very governmental inefficiency we complain about is the salvation of the system,

The most efficient form of government is a dictatorship. Whether you agree with that or not depends upon which side of the dictator you find yourself. If you and the dictator agree, you're "in tall cotton," as they would say down in Oklahoma. "Tall Cotton;" that means you don't have to bend over and break your back to pick the cotton bolls, they're all up high and – well – I stray from my story but the metaphor is a good one. If you don't agree with the dictator his problem is a simple one. It's "Off mitt the head." Once more everyone agrees with the dictator. That system was efficient and worked pretty well. Ask Saddam Hussein.

Democracy is known to be slow and cumbersome and inefficient but therein is the very safety of the system. No individual can do anything suddenly; no one can "off mitt the head." There's got to be an agreement, a decision made by the many including you and I through our elected representatives. This awkward, cumbersome, ponderous and unwieldy system has lasted for over 200 years and is still going strong. The pendulum has swung from "liberal" to "conservative" and in between over the years and probably wavered toward other stranger views along the way. But the system of checks and balances created by our founders has produced the greatest nation on earth.

Newspapers and television play upon the sensational, emphasize the lurid, suggest the unanswered question, the embarrassing or catastrophic. When things are running smoothly that's not news. Too many of us are quick to believe the sensational and may add our voice to the general condemnation. And so many of us who complain the loudest about elected officials didn't bother vote in the last election.

The majority of government employees at all levels, hired, appointed or elected, are doing the best job that they know how. They may have a bad day now and then but don't we all? They don't always agree with what I think should be done but that's the way the system works. I would like to believe they might have a deeper knowledge of the problems than I do – at least I sincerely hope they do. If a majority of us come to disagree we can "throw the bum out." We can vote them out but only if we fulfill our democratic responsibility by voting. So everything that happens in this country of ours is our responsibility, yours and mine.

You know, I sometimes wonder why anyone wants to be a politician. Would you trade places with any of them? Would you like to be the President of the United States? Is it a power thing that attracts people? Or is it an urge to try to make things better? Look at photographs of those we elect as they serve over the years they're in office. You can see them aging, sagging, wearing down under the responsibilities. And think for a minute of all the political maneuvering, the electioneering, the gut-level disagreement they might feel while still smiling and shaking hands and trying not to alienate someone. And, have you noticed, they all seem to develop the ability to talk at great length leaving a listener with a favorable impression but without having answered the question at all? It would seem our system is a real mess, isn't it?

CR

"You" is the first letter in U.S.A.

CR

Merry Christmas GI Style

As a local author I regularly donate my books to the Jacobetti Veteran's Home. Being a veteran myself I subscribe to the attitude I recently heard expressed on a military "shoot 'em up" television program. One soldier was asked by another why he had done such-and-such for another soldier, "a stranger." The man paused, looked his questioner in the eye, and replied, "He's not a stranger. He's one of us." And that's the way it is.

One day Jacobetti Activities Aid Randy Satio bumped into me in the hall. He mentioned that the weight of the years on many of the residents was making it difficult or impossible for them to read, even the large type with which my books are printed. They had been asking Randy if he would please read the books to them. My immediate thought was that that kind of appreciation of my efforts was the genuine article and not easily obtained.

That encounter launched me on a program to create an audio version of my latest book, "Life is Not a Destination." A few months later, with the audio version published and available on the market, I was eager to donate it to the fella's (and ladies) at the Jacobetti Center.

Wouldn't you just know it? Another obstacle arose.

They had no access to a CD player. Another old soldiering expression came to mind: "There's no way we're quittin' 'til we win the war." Having come this far that little "no CD player" glitch wasn't going to stop us. I bought a couple CD players and packaged the players and the audio books into Christmas presents for fellow veterans Marvin Thompson and Eino Numela. "Merry Christmas, fella's! Share 'em with the troops!"

As I was leaving, bubbling over with the Christmas spirit, I once again encountered Randy Satio. "Merry Christmas, Randy! I've just made your life a little easier." When I told him of the gift of the CDs and the CD player he said, "Oh, No! I was enjoying reading your stories as much as they were listening." How about that? There are some days when, no matter what you do, you just can't seem to win. But, on second thought, I think maybe I did win - twice? What do you think?

I didn't let all this go to my head though. When I got home I told Dorothy she didn't have to call me "Sir" – unless, of course, there were strangers around.

☙

Let's Go Hunting

Hunting has evolved over the passing years and many of us wonder if it should still be called hunting? Baiting, even with salt blocks was once illegal. The reasons for hunting's evolution can be cussed and discussed and argued for and against. Many say the practice of baiting has come about because of the loss of free ranging areas open to the average hunter. Others point out that the time constraints of today's fast-paced society don't allow the leisurely paced sport of the old days; that there are "more efficient" hunting methods. Instead of a hunter searching for the game, they should entice the game to come to the hunter. That'll solve the lack of land to roam problem and, by planning ahead and establishing bait piles in advance, will also reduce the time spent waiting. I wonder if these ideas aren't from the same people who introduced artificial insemination? Well, as they say, 'different strokes for different folks.' If that's the way they want it, who am I to argue? If, on the other hand, you are someone who enjoys a walk in the woods, the beauty of a sunset, the wonder of a wild-flower, you're my kinda people. Read on.

The creatures that live in the forests have a pretty tough life. Their whole existence is comprised of searching for food, sleeping, breeding in season and staying alive. To hunt them, to go out in search of them, to outsmart them in their own realm dictates that you know a little about them. The more you know the better. If you've read the stories in the "macho" outdoor magazines you'll have come to one of two conclusions: you'll be so intimidated by the skill and cunning attributed to the story's author that you may decide to take up knitting. The other conclusion is that you'll recognize the story you're reading – and I'm being kind here – has been embellished maybe just a little. Let's ash can some of those magazine articles and take a walk in the woods ourselves.

Animals live out their whole lives in a relatively small section of the woods. They know the area like the back of their paw or their hoof. Many of their senses are far superior to yours and mine. A bear may not be able to see as well as you and I but its sense of smell may be telling it a whole lot more than we can see with our eyes. An owl's eyes are fixed in their sockets. It has to turn its whole head to look in another direction but its hearing exceeds ours by a multiple of a hundred or more, even on our best days. The eyes of an eagle have what we'd call a binocular ability to look down from a couple thousand feet and see a tiny mouse hiding under a leaf. It's been said, "If a leaf falls in the forest, the eagle will see it fall, the deer will hear it fall and the bear will smell it." There's more truth than "just cute" to that statement.

If you're going to hunt those creatures – I wouldn't

guess you'd be hunting owls but you get the idea – don't try to beat in areas where they are far superior to you. Folks who subscribe to the theory of evolution tell us that we humans have grown to be more intelligent, smarter than the animals. You, like me, might have times when you question that but let's let it pass for now. We can't move through the woods so quietly that they won't hear you but try to be quiet enough not to alarm them. You can't move so slowly that they won't see you but slow movement is not so startling. You can't, even by avoiding perfume and aftershave, render yourself so odor free that they won't smell you. Think about those things and how you can minimize their effect.

Don't hunt downwind. Your odor travels with the wind, even a slight breeze, so anything downwind of you will know all about you. Move slowly with frequent stops to look all around. You should spend more time looking than moving – and know that moving your head as you look is "moving." Also keep in mind the gun you're carrying. You may not be moving your arm or hand much but the barrel or butt of your gun may be moving quite a bit. Here's another point. I've watched a hunter climbing a hill, grasping a small sapling to help them up. Then they'll crouch and creep to the crest and peek over. They're hoping to surprise something, to catch some critter unaware. Next time you grab a sapling, look at the upper branches. They're waving around like a flag on the fourth of July. Fat chance you're going to surprise anything that way.

If you elect to stand someplace where you can watch a game trail, pick a spot downwind, a spot where you will blend in behind a bush or by standing close up to a large tree trunk. Once you're there, don't move anything but your eyeballs. An animal knows this environment and will notice any change. It may even notice that that tree trunk is suddenly fatter than it was the last time it passed this way. Those are the skills and abilities that have allowed it to stay alive, to grow that rack of horns you may be coveting. Death is a constant companion to creatures in the wild and they've learned to live with it. Truth be known death is a closer companion than we care to acknowledge too. It's always there. Don't forget that.

Well, I'm out of space. If you'd like to talk some more like this, maybe we can another time. If I've offered you a little something to think about, that's great. If you don't think much of my ideas, well, that'll have to be OK too.

CR

Northbound

    I just watched a line of geese, oh, it must have been at least three miles long fly over. They were a couple thousand feet up in the air strung out over the village of Harvey and headed north across the big lake, Lake Superior. The first thing that had caught my attention was that familiar distant muttering sound. That sound always seems to come across as if several people off in the distance somewhere were all speaking at the same time. A person can hear them talking but you can't make out what they're saying. If you buy that talking idea and substituted geese for persons I think the description is accurate.

There's something about geese that holds a strong – I don't know – a bond, a brotherly or sisterly feeling. I don't know if this next is bragging or complaining but I, too, have spent a good bit of my life moving from one place to another. I guess it's natural instinct for the geese. I haven't yet found an excuse for myself. There's a lot to admire about the geese even though they poop indiscriminately all over our dock and our wooden deck and throughout Dorothy's flower garden. We elect upstanding and righteous citizens locally and send them to Lansing and Washington D.C. Frequently we find they aren't any more discriminating than the geese. In Dorothy's garden I tell her that's what makes the flowers grow. Have you noticed how often those politicians seem to be telling us the same thing?

When spring comes once again to our north country and I hear that distant muttering I just have to stop whatever I'm doing and listen and look. That sight and the sound kind of mesmerize me. I stare up at that wavering formation, listen to their muttering and wonder what they're saying to one another? I understand it's usually a female, a goose that leads the flight. Maybe that's got something to do with the male ego and his inclination to never stop and ask directions? It's probably more to do with the female finding a safe, secure and familiar nesting site to raise the family.

Ducks, especially the mallards, always remind me

of the guys who hang around the bars on pay day nights. A male duck, a drake, is very attentive for the breeding but then he's off to hang around with other drakes the rest of the year. I imagine those drakes talking about the great things they're going to do "one of these days" - just like those guys at the bar. Meanwhile, back at the nest, that hen has to tend the home, feed and clothe the young and teach them the ways of the world. The burden of the future rests on the shoulders of the female – just like with us. She's gotta take the scraps the male may brings home and stretch it and make-do to cover the families needs. Some of you hangers-on at the bar oughta be ashamed of yourselves. Maybe that has something to do with why you stop in the bar in the first place?

The gander, the male goose is not so inclined. When the female is on the nest the gander stays nearby, guard duty you might call it. Any creature – including you or I – who thinks that's just for show is apt to get a rude surprise.

Maybe, as I watch at that flight of geese soaring high overhead, I'm a bit jealous. Maybe, compared to that gander's fidelity, I feel I may be lacking something. I heard a story of a faithful gander that, when the goose was injured and unable to fly, refused to join the other geese in their flight south that fall. He stayed with his mate. Thanks to the care and consideration of a neighboring farmer that pair survived the winter sheltered in his shed. He passed their story on to me.

That other thing we associate with the geese; if we

were a little more inclined that way we may not need so many remedies for the relief of constipation and other stomach upsets. Maybe we should all feel freer to - HOOONK! Golldarn it! I pretty near got run over. Stopping in the middle of the driveway of a gasoline station to watch and listen to geese is probably not a smart thing to do. One last glance upward at that wavering line of northbound geese, another toward the irate driver who seems to think my mother ate table scraps and slept under the porch and I, too, travel a little north – at least out of the way of that automobile.

CR

Sittin' by the Fire

We had a couple of really cold days there. Not being inclined in that weather to step outside to sunbathe, I sat inside with a hot cup of coffee. I would have gone out but as cold as it was, whenever I'd move or roll over the snow would squeak and that kept me awake. Are you buying this up to here? I didn't think so. Anyway, the part about inside and the hot coffee is true.

Some of the people who attend craft shows and were kind enough to stop by my little book-peddling booth had expressed an interest in a book containing some of the older articles I had written. I've been assembling some of those stories during the cold weather when those of us who are sane are staying indoors. You're holding the result in your hands. At my present age and reviewing recollections from the past, the coffee tends to grow cold in the cup as my mind drifts. I know what some of you are thinking about that last remark there but you just leave it alone. You're going to get old yourself one day.

Anyway, looking back and wondering, you know, what would have happened if I had turned left instead of right back there when - - well, you get the idea, I was over in Viet Nam with a young fella – younger than I was – who was my "back-seater" in an F-4 fighter bomber. I drove the machine but Lipper, operated the electronic systems in the back seat and kept an eye on me. Lipper and I were a team. His appropriate comments and timely advice brushed the angel of death off of us more than once.

There's a bond that forms between people – men - women too, I assume – when they have "walked through the valley of the shadow" together. Lipper was a good man to stand with.

Back to happier thoughts and philosophies discovered along the way. If you live right, enjoy each day, love children, and maintain respect for your fellow man you'll never be sorry you came. Mark Twain put it very well: "Live a life so that when you die, even the undertaker will be sorry you're gone."

You can blame all my morose recollections on that disease they have discovered called "SAD." I'm not sure what that acronym stands for but it has something to do with this time of year and the lack of sunshine and an inclination to kick the dog.

We're brought into this world not by choice but by chance. You had nothing to say about whom your parents would be or what country or social strata you would be born into. Once here, you live by choice – your choice. You can judge the glass half full or half empty, the call is yours. If you happen to have been born "with a silver spoon in your mouth" or achieved good fortune through personal effort, chance had a hand in placing you in that situation, with giving you the "smart" to take advantage of it. Don't presume to look down on anybody. In the end that's all there is - the end.

Here's another quotation, something Albert Einstein once said that's worth thinking about over coffee: Darn! My cup has gone cold. "The only life worth while is a life lived for others." Life is not a destination – it's what you do along the way.

Hey! Whaddya know! The sun just came out! Let's go get a little sunshine.

CR

Good judgment comes from experience
Experience comes from bad judgment.

CR

Some Assembly Required

"Insert Tab A into Slot B." Do you remember the

days when these were the instructions that came with purchases in which "some assembly" was required? Boy! Are those days ever gone and forgotten. To be strictly fair, maybe the troubles I'm having with modern day "assembly" are partly me too. I find myself going into the basement, for example, and once there, wondering what it was I went down there to get?

With my hearing fading a bit, from listening to too many jet engines they tell me, I bought one of those "stereophonic home-theater surround-sound" things to hook up to the "High Definition Television" set complete with VCR and DVD. I anticipated entering the total entertainment environment of our modern world. Yeah! Tell me about it. I removed the back of the TV – DVD – etc. cabinet filled with confidence and high expectation. I soon found myself in an electronic nightmare from hell. "To connect the digital . . . Video 1, Video 2, Video3 . . . coaxial . . . optical input jack . . . change the assignment of . . . an S Video terminal." Where are tab A and tab B? There's a bold print highlighted notice: "DO NOT connect the power cord at this time." Slow as I am I could understand the reasoning behind that warning.

I dug into the instructions again. Some of the directions were obviously written by someone not all that familiar with English in its America-Speak form. It may take a bit of imagination to understand what was written and even then a person is not sure. I had invested thirty-two dollars and some odd cents in a couple of "S" video cables that are supposed to "greatly improve" picture quality. I plugged them in here and there and somewhere else that looked appropriate. There was no picture at all. I finally stumbled across a note to a note that said, in effect, "You can't get there from here" – my equipment, even though it had the terminals, was not compatible with that type hook-up. Sheeesh!

While in the military I once heard a story about "Napoleon's Captain." Never mind if it's true or not, it's a good story and makes a point we too often overlook. It was said that Napoleon gave an intelligence test to everyone in his army. When he had identified the, what's a nice way to put this, the "least intelligent" individual, he promoted him to the rank of Captain. (Never mind all you wiseacres who are saying they're still doing that.) Napoleon made this new Captain his personal aid and took him everywhere he went. When Napoleon issued an order to units of his army he first gave it to this Captain and asked him what the order said. When that Captain could understand it correctly, Napoleon would send it out to the rest of his army. If any of you electronics producers out there should read this, I may be the man qualified to be your personal aid.

At least I haven't blown out any fuses nor caught anything on fire. I did finally muster the courage to connect the power cord. I know the question that must be on all your minds: Is the thing working? I gotta tell you, I don't know. We can switch channels. The sounds we get are often not associated at all with the picture we're seeing but, sometimes, they seem to be "stereophonic."

Of course there are an armload of remote controllers for all these devices and the sound-picture combinations often depend on which controller I am attempting to use at the moment.

In frustration I take a break now and then and go outside and split a little firewood. Inserting blade "A" into block "B" is a little easier to understand. I get a feeling of accomplishment, a feeling that I have been able to do something useful when that firewood splits.

Meanwhile, Dorothy is in the house watching a Redwings hockey game on the television while hearing The News Hour with Jim Lehrer coming through the audio – but it's delivered in the latest five-speaker high fidelity stereophonic surround sound (I think).

CR

Spring has Sprung

Earlier, toward the end of March, a couple of Canadian Geese landed on the bayou. Not "in" the bayou but "on" the bayou. The whole darn bayou was still frozen over. Ice! Snow! No open water anywhere. We've had a pair of geese that have nested with us every year and raised their chicks on the bayou. Are these the same pair? From their attitude, just the way they act I'm guessing they are. Showing up so early, before the anticipated St. Patrick day's blizzard and all, I was inclined to think they might have gotten into somebody's marijuana patch on their way north. The snow and ice didn't seem to bother them though. They wandered through the frozen marsh evidently looking for a suitable nesting site. I wish them luck but I suspect they're smarter in matters like that than I am.

Thinking about their situation I realize their schedule is pretty tight. They've got to build – or rebuild – a nest site, lay half dozen or so eggs and incubate them for about 30 days. Once the goslings have hatched they've got the whole of the goose education to teach them. Both goose and gander are dedicated to and share the care for the chicks. Woe be to whoever or whatever may attempt to harm them or, earlier, to threaten the nest. A goose can weigh up to twenty pounds or so and those wings are strong enough to propel it at speeds up to sixty miles an hour. Any intruder will meet an attack and a beating from those wings.

The gander is faithful to his mate for life. He doesn't leave to go philandering as Mallard Ducks are wont to do. In spite of their tendency to let their bowels function without regard to where they happen to be there are many traits to admire in those geese. And there are probably some of us who would wish our bowels would work so well.

I was concerned that they may have been crowding the season, that they would be caught in a late spring blizzard. I was concerned that is until just this morning. My change of heart didn't have anything to do with our TV weather forecaster. Whenever our local weatherman comes on wearing a long face and a subdued manner you know the weather is going to be good. When he's all excited and waving his pointer at his charts you know he's got a storm up his sleeve somewhere. No, the thing that eased my concerns for the welfare of the geese scurried past my window just this morning.

You see, Dorothy and I feed "the critters" pretty regularly. We may miss a morning or two, maybe we're visiting out of town or maybe we just forgot. The daily feedings are regular enough that the ducks and geese and squirrels and, well, every critter around are usually out there waiting for us. We even had one seagull that would boldly land on the back porch, walk up to the sliding glass door, and knock on the glass with its bill to remind us that it was feeding time. We generally feed pretty well. There's sunflower seed in "Levi and Hudson's Diner," a bird feeder labeled for our grandkids who enjoy watching. Whole corn is scattered from the porch into (or onto) the Bayou. Day-old bread gets broken up and scattered around for the seagulls and anything else that's interested. We have peanuts in the shell that are of particular interest to the squirrels and the blue jays. Dorothy maintains the thistle feeders for goldfinches and their friends. A couple nuthatches come by to examine a block of suet. We enjoy watching our "critters," feed, watch them chase each other and otherwise cavort around. Watching all this activity, I sometimes suspect we may be feeding the animals better than we're feeding ourselves. And then I climb on the bathroom scale and it tells me I may be eating a bit more than I should.

Back to the "scurry by the window" weather forecast that bolstered my belief in an early spring. It was a chipmunk. It was exploring, searching for a snack I would guess.

Chipmunks hibernate for the winter upon the arrival of the first snow. They don't show themselves again 'til spring. I say "hibernate" a little quickly but they do retreat to their burrows. The burrow may have a sleeping area, a food storage area and even a bathroom area. For all I know they even stay up to catch the late news on the TV. Anyway, that chipmunk was up and about. It must be spring.

The Adventure

Spring (maybe that was summer?) seemed to come on like gangbusters this year. There was no St. Patrick's Day storm or – what did you say? What's gangbusters? Well back in those past golden days beyond recall there was a radio program that – no, no you can't get it on an I-pod. It was – oh, heck, just ask someone with a little silver in their hair - or very little hair left. They'll tell you about gangbusters.

Anyway, spring seemed to come on suddenly. On a trip to Big Bay the snow in the woods was ---by its absence. It was very little or no snow to be seen anywhere!

And this was only April! I made a mental note that, if I finished my business in Bay Bay early enough, I would drive in to my camp on the Yellow Dog River. I hadn't been there since last fall. Every spring I approach my old cabin, the cabin that Tom "Tin Can" Sullivan built back about 1927, the one the years have given a sway-back to the roof, and dread that I will see it fallen in. Every spring it lives on like the legend of Tom himself. One spring, in spite of my propping and bracing, it will have given up the ghost – literally. Tom shot himself up in that old cabin. And sometimes, on a clear quiet summer evening with a full moon shining down, a person can talk to ole Tom. He doesn't say much though. As matter of fact he never did. But I digress. Back to the "Adventure."

I finished up in Big Bay early. I was pushing a bit so it was earlier than normal. With the lack of apparent snow I thought I would drive in to the cabin "the long way," the scenic route and see how the two rut roads had weathered the winter. I wasn't more than a quarter mile from the main road when I first hit mud. I vaguely entertained the thought of turning around as the mud seemed churned up by more traffic than I remembered using that road. Instead I got out, locked the front hubs and shifted into four wheel drive. I had watched the TV ads and knew that with four wheel drive I could climb mountains, swim oceans, spin around on the bare road and perform other deeds of daring do. I was invincible!

The little tracker threw a little mud and bounced a bit but we made it through. At about a half or three quarters of a mile there was more mud. This was on a slope, uphill, and I took a bit of a run at it. Good thing! I feared a time or two I wasn't going to make it. I wonder if those guys who make those advertisements have ever been in Upper Michigan in the spring? The trail still showed signs of rather heavy traffic that puzzled me some. There were no hunting seasons currently open. Trout fishing wouldn't start 'til the last Saturday in April. Who is doing all the driving in the woods?

Mamma Mia! There's another stretch of mud. Tracks indicated that others had passed this way throwing mud and fish-tailing and – well – pedal to the metal and here I go. Correction! Here I didn't go! You know, in these situations there's usually a little bit of lurching back and forth before you are convinced that you're stuck. Not so in this case. That little four-wheel drive GEO Tracker had sunk into the mud immediately and so deep I had trouble getting the door open to get out. I waded around the car digging under seats and through bags and boxes searching for some help in this predicament and found absolutely nothing. I glanced upward a time or two hoping for a little guidance but I fear He was looking down and laughing at me.

After a brief, futile and frustrating few minutes trying to come up with some plan for redemption I accepted the situation and began contemplating what to do next. It would be a couple miles walking back out the road. It'd be a bit more than that if I continued the way I was headed. What the heck. I'm supposed to be somewhat of a woodsman. After all, I write those stories don't I? Lessee, the sun is in the south – a little west of south. If I keep the sun over my right shoulder I'll be going east and run into the road that goes around Bear Lake maybe three quarters of a mile away. Here I go!

I should take the keys so no one can steal the car? Hah! If they can drive it out of that mud hole, they can have it.

Hiking around the occasional patch of snow, choosing the easier path around the brush and rocks I couldn't help wondering why the darn sun had moved out of the southwest. Put the sun back over my right shoulder and press on.

Suddenly there is a woods road and an eight or ten block basement/foundation that's big enough to be a basketball court. This is in the middle of the woods! I used to hunt through here – get lost wandering around here. And now someone is building a high rise apartment building? Sheesh!

Continuing with the sun, the shoulder and onward I came to the Bear Lake Road – and there was a cabin – and another – and. There are a whole bunch of cabins here that I don't remember seeing before. Golly! Maybe this is a village I didn't know about? Looking for some help I knocked on the door. No answer. I try the knob. The door's open. "Hellooo?" No one's home. Go to the next cabin. Same thing.

I hike the road around the lake. I know a fella who

lives there with his wife year 'round. As I approach his home the dogs raise a ruckus. They're barking but their tails are wagging. A scratch behind the ears and I've made a friend. His basement door is open wide with his pickup truck is backed up to it. The tail gate is open. Hope surges. Here is some help. Wrong! Nobody home here either. Two more places I stopped had no one home. One place even had the door wide open. Finally I'm back on the highway.

Start walking toward Big Bay about five miles or so away. A car comes along. My thumb goes out. The cars goes by. Maybe that was someone from the Huron Mountain Club. You gotta excuse them. They're from the city. Along comes a pickup truck and I've got a ride. It's big. It's new. It's four-wheel drive. And in spite of my woeful tale it's not going up into the woods to pull me out either. I'll bet the underside of this truck is still show-room clean. Don't bitch! The guy gave me a ride!

I get out at the Big Bay Outfitters. They're still closed as their season hasn't started yet but I lucked out. Bill Kinjorski is working inside. When he hears my sad tale he immediately saddles up in his truck. He and I and his son, "Terrible Tom," head for the outback. (Terrible Tom is three years old. Bill has been baby sitting.)

Guess what. Bill gets stuck in that first mud hole just a quarter mile in. We (Bill and another fella who happens along) crawl around in the mud and shovel and twist and rationalize. Terrible Tom and I watch but have sense enough not to make suggestions. Soon we're out and on up the road albeit it more carefully – more carefully or more aggressively, one or the other – and arrive at the scene of my demise. Under the supervision of Terrible Tom we were soon out of mud and headed back toward the highway. We went through the same mud holes but down hill this time and, you know, careful – aggressive, maybe both.

"Bill, how much do I owe you?" "Forget it. You'd do the same for me." Isn't Big Bay a great place to live?

"The Deal!"

Greg Lindstrom and his 1924 Model "T" Ford

"You can have 'er for $35.00.

"Geez! That's a bit much."

Enter the Lee Iacocca philosophy into this negotiation - "the most important part - the deal!" "If you can find a better car . . ." Well, perhaps we'd better leave Lee's philosophy at "the deal" for reasons that will soon be apparent. This little scenario was played out, lessee, I'd guess it must have been about June – in 1954.

Greg Lindstrom had just graduated from High School. Johnnie Letts had been living in Oregon and had come to Upper Michigan, got a job and was intending to stay. Here's what the situation was at that moment: Greg, a proud new High School graduate, had received $15.00 in graduation money – total – period. The police on the other hand had just informed our recent Upper Michigan immigrant, Johnnie, that since he was now employed in Michigan he had to get a Michigan license plate to replace the Oregon plate for the vehicle he was presently driving (not the vehicle in question) – immediately. His other vehicle, the one on which the negotiation centered, was a 1924 Model "T" Ford. This was the machine that was owned by Johnnie and coveted by Greg.

The two negotiators circled one another probing and testing for possible advantage. The one was limited by circumstances to a maximum of fifteen dollars while the other was looking down the barrel of a policeman's gun, so to speak, for nine dollars to purchase a license plate. After circling and eyeing one another, hands in pockets, scuffing the dirt with a toe, probably spitting a time or two as was acceptable during negotiating in those days, a sale price of fifteen dollars was agreed upon.

Now came another glitch. The seller needed the money – all of it – right now! The buyer didn't have all the money with him "right now." The State of Michigan doesn't take IOUs for a license plate.

Faced with this new dilemma, a lesser man may have accepted defeat and withdrew. But Greg Lindstrom was not "a lesser man." He was also in the company of friends. He and Dick Lutey, Dick Hendra, Melvin and "Peanuts" Sweeney dug into their pockets, pooled their resources and came up with the necessary fifteen dollars. Johnnie was soon on his way to buy a license plate and Greg was the proud owner of brand new and . . uh . . beautiful . . . Well, it wasn't brand new. Truth be known, it wasn't too beautiful either. You've heard the expression, "a face only a mother could love"? Well, consider Greg to be the mother. The model "T" had four flat tires. Sometime in the distant past it had been painted barn-red by someone with more enthusiasm than skill wielding what must have been a somewhat tired and not-too-neat paintbrush. What's more the engine didn't run. The convertible top and the interior upholstery, well, the kindest thing to say is it was not. There was no upholstery or top. So much for Lee Iacoca's "if you can find a better car" ploy.

When Greg's mother discovered what he had done with his graduation money – ALL his graduation money – she seriously questioned "the deal" part too. She also might have wondered if her son had been playing football without a helmet. Such are the trials and tribulations of parenting.

To bring the story up to date, that poor old model "T" has experienced a large dose of tender loving care over the years since that day back in 1954. Greg Lindstrom still owns it. You'd hardly recognize it today for the car it was back then. You can come and take a look too, if you want. I'll tell you how in a minute.

You see Greg is not alone in his addiction to renovating things old and decrepit. A local group of like-minded individuals gathers at various places on uncertain dates to swap stories similar to this one you just read. They appreciate the "old days" and the old cars and enjoy getting together and reminiscing. I met Greg at such a gathering held in the parking lot of Applebee's Restaurant one Saturday afternoon. There were a total of 43 old cars and their owners there – give or take. The ladies are represented in this group too. Everyone is welcome. Just watch the newspaper for the time and place of their next meeting. Stop by. Look over the machines. Listen to the stories. Enjoy.

CR

The Golden Times

I stood at the kitchen window looking out across the bayou. The sun was up –just enough to accent the golden colors tinting the surrounding trees. Early mornings are a wonder filled time of day. You know, when I was just a young fella working at an hourly wage I could never seem to get to work on time. The old Cliffs Dow Chemical Company was still in operation belching out smoke and charcoal and that familiar "eau de chemical wood" odor that was so familiar on the north side of Marquette back then. I'd punch the clock three or four or five minutes late. The company would dock me for fifteen minutes. My cousin Fred, who worked in the office at the time, would see my time card and give me h—l. He was an accountant and would explain to me how much it was costing me over a week or two. It didn't do any good.

Now, when I can sleep 'til noon if I want to, I'm usually up and around anytime from 4:00 AM on. Whaddya make of that?

Anyway, I was looking out across the bayou. Ducks and the geese were already assembled waiting for me to feed them. I was just enjoying being alive. Those birds come right up to the dock; close enough that I (and my grandsons when they're with me) could almost pat them on the head. Just couple miles away hunters hide in blinds, paint their faces with elaborate camouflage, serenade them with expensive duck-calls and can't entice them close enough to take a shot. I try to tell Dorothy they come to me because I'm so good lookin'. She just gives me one of those sideways looks with which we long suffering handsome husbands are so familiar. My wife just doesn't understand me – or maybe understands too well?

Fall is fast coming on, our golden time of the year, and partridge hunters are afield. It's always amazed me how a partridge would flush right in front of me then manage to get a tree between it and myself. That seemed pretty clever.

I remember one night – black dark – my little truck had broken down a couple miles from the cabin. By looking overhead at the slightly lighter night sky and with what familiarity I had with that section of woods and trails I was able to follow the truck trail back to camp. While I was stumbling along there was a sudden explosion right under my feet. My eyes popped wide open. What hair I still have stood straight up. That which hadn't yet turned white did so immediately. A partridge had "blown up" right under my feet. I fumbled with a flashlight, switched it on, and there was this indignant bird, just three or four feet away looking very haughtily at me. It acted like the whole thing was my fault – and I guess it was. But that bird obviously couldn't see much better than I could. It had flown right into a bush and was now indignantly re-arranging its ruffled feathers. We looked at each other. I apologized. It evidently accepted my apology. We each went our separate ways.

Another story I remember has been told and retold but it's worth telling again. Jack Andersen, partridge hunting with a friend, was enjoying the fall color and the outdoors along a two-rut back-woods road. Suddenly there was a partridge just ahead on Jack's side of the road. It would be Jack's shot. He fumbled around loading his gun getting ready to shoot. Nothing happened. "Shoot! Shoot!" his partner hissed impatiently.

"I can't! I can't!" Jack whispered back.

"Why?"

"I got Tums in my gun!"

Now that's an answer you don't often hear. What

do you make of that? Being told a hunting story like that and then left hanging is almost enough to turn a person away from his Christian upbringing. Well, I had a Christian upbringing too so I'll explain.

Jack had an upset stomach, a little stomach acidity probably, and had been taking Tums. He had put the roll of tums in his jacket pocket – along with his shotgun shells. "Now you know the rest of the story" – don't you? In his haste he stuffed the roll of Tums into the gun rather than a shell. Jack may still be having acidity problems but they're probably because none of us will let him forget about loading his shotgun with ant-acid tablets.

Pause for a moment and review all the fun and adventure you and I have just had – and we haven't yet left the kitchen. Guys – and girls – who've hauled themselves out of bed and into the woods at this early hour couldn't possibly be enjoying their day more than you and I - and we're still drinking our first cup of cof-fee. Yes, I guess these truly are the Golden Times. It's a great world we're living in, isn't it?

CR

Trick or Treat

If you go out in the dark tonight, you're in for a big surprise. If you go out in the dark tonight, you'd better go in disguise, 'cause goblins and ghosties and ghoulies galore will be crossing streets running from door to door – and they probably won't be watching for traffic. This is a big night for them. Their attention will be on treats and goodies and they'll be hurrying to get more. They won't be watching for the comings and goings of cars and trucks and other things that go 'bump' in the night. You and I'll have to cut 'em a little slack on this special night. And keep in mind it can be difficult for them to see from inside those "skulls" and from under those witch's hats. It'll be up to us to add that extra ration of "careful" to our driving, just for them.

Aah, it's a great time of life to be that young and carefree. The baggage of the adult world has not yet settled on their shoulders and creased their brows with concern. Preoccupation with the cares of tomorrow and next month and Iraq and the United Nations and on and on is still a long way off. Look into those laughing faces, the excitement reflected in their eyes and remember the old days – and enjoy it all again.

Outhouses were a tempting target for us kids back in the old days. Today kids probably don't know what an outhouse is and that, too, is a good thing. I remember one dark Halloween night we snuck up on an outhouse. Just as we were putting our shoulders to tipping it over, someone sitting inside (I assume they were sitting?) burst out the door holding their britches up with one hand. Those lowered britches probably saved us. We took off running and our "victim" couldn't run fast enough to catch us. This happened out in the country, out in Harvey. Harvey, in those days, was small enough that who we were was probably suspected but large enough that they couldn't be sure.

Swiping apples was a deed of daring back then but folks had so many apple trees they didn't seem to pay any attention. You know the apple trees are still out there. They're not tended as well as they used to be in the old days. In fact most of them are not tended at all. They just grow wild, blossom, are pollinated by passing bees, bear their fruit and drop it on the ground. This time of year deer hunters might scavenge them for a bait pile. They'll be "deer apples" rather than apples they'll eat themselves.

I'm going to tell you a little secret here – call it my "trick or treat" goodie to you for the season. To many of you senior citizens, especially the ladies, this may not be a secret but work with me here. I have a weakness for apple pies. I dearly love a good apple pie. Back in the days when I was single and tending to my own needs I could bake a pretty mean apple pie. I bought the shell at the grocery but I mixed the innards myself. There are recipes galore and, for my apple pies, one recipe was probably about as good as another. So what's the secret, you ask? The secret is the apples.

I wander a bit in the bushes and along the back roads in the area. It's surprising all the places you'll find an apple tree. There's got to be two of them, actually, the one is necessary to cross-pollinate the other. In the woods they probably mark the area of a long-ago logging camp. Some trees are growing and bearing their fruit right alongside the road – a side road, that is. Anyway, I sample their fruit in season. A whole lot of these apples were rather bland or small or hard and not worth bothering with. But every now and then I'd discover a real jewel among all the chaff. One such tree was out along Mangum Road, south of Marquette. It was growing beside the road right in the fence line so I didn't feel I was stealing. I only took a few apples anyway, just enough for a pie.

Writing this, I can taste those pies again. I haven't been back for a while now; Dorothy takes care of the kitchen these days. She and daughter, Mary, have me on a pretty short "weight control" leash. I wonder if that tree is still there? And still bearing fruit? Dorothy may go to a Redwings Hockey game in Detroit for a couple days. I could probably duck Mary for a day or two. How can I share this treat with grandsons Levi and Hudson without their momma finding out? I've gotta work on that.

So – accept this "selective wild-apple-pie recipe" as my "treat" at this season of the year. And watch out for those little goblins that will be cluttering up the roads.

CR

TV or Not TV

When I was a kid – now you younger folks have learned to kind of turn off, shut down when an older person prefaces a comment with "When I was – whatever." I guess I used to do that too – still do. The trouble is it's getting harder and harder to find someone older than myself. When you find yourself checking the obituaries in the evening paper before turning to the comics it means you're approaching being older than dirt – and maybe not too far from returning to it.

Anyway, after checking the obituaries, I checked the TV schedule. In our capitalistic system it's the commercials that sponsor the television entertainment. The entertainment is aimed at an audience that has the money and the inclination to make the purchases touted in the commercials. Evidently their target audience does not include me. That's what makes the world go 'round though and I guess it's as it should be. The fliers in the newspaper, commercials on television, posters along the highways and the elaborate displays in our vast "I need a roadmap to find my way around" department stores, I am amazed at the number of things I can live very comfortably without. And they're getting to be three or six levels deep in these things. Buy this because it automates something else you don't really need making it work that much easier – unless you breath, sleep or take nutrients in which case consult your doctor first.

When I was a kid – there it goes again. When I was, oh, this memory dates back - I must have been under ten years old. We were still living on Michigan Street in town. My great grandmother was living with us. She must have been a couple hundred years old at least – older than dirt, you know. Families took in and looked after their own seniors back then. Anyway, I remember coming home in the evening and grandma would be sitting alone in the dark in the living room. There was no TV – I think we did have a radio but she seldom listened to it. Grandma would be sitting in the dark, rocking slightly in her old rocking chair. Sometimes she'd be talking to herself, not loud but soft and low and nodding her head in agreement with whatever she was saying. She spoke German more readily than she spoke English and that added to the mystique in my young mind. I remember it scaring me a little. Who was she talking to? Now that I am approaching that "older than dirt" stage myself I think I might know.

We have so much to distract us these days, to occupy our every waking moment that we don't have time to think or reflect or reminisce anymore. The TV is on or the radio is blaring or the I-pod is plugged into your ear and all of it is vying for attention and saturating your senses with sound. How often do we have the TV or the radio on and we aren't watching or even listening. It was just something to be there. You weren't alone.

Well grandma didn't have any of those things but she wasn't alone either. I think I understand it a little better now. I often find myself sitting alone in a dark room these days. I'm not talking to myself yet but that'll probably come. There'll be a fire in the fireplace and I'll be watching the flames. Do you realize that that flickering firelight is older than – or at least as old as – dirt? Looking there I see a campfire in the woods. There's a kid with a charred old frying pan making pancakes for his father. Dad worked the night shift on the Marquette Police Force but he would often forego sleep the next day in order to take his young son, me, hunting. Tired as he was he'd often fall asleep lying on a pine branch pallet I would have made against a fallen log. The log would reflect the heat of the fire making the pallet warm and comfortable. Then I'd wake him up to eat pancakes. He never complained. You see, for me there was a better program in the fireplace than there was on TV.

I guess that's what great grandma was doing too. Those memories were better programs than on TV or the radio. Memories are things you younger folks don't have – not yet anyway. I like to think my father knew that I appreciated him and the things he did without just for me. Maybe you younger folks can think about that. It's the things we do for others that will live long after we're gone. In the dark, by myself, I realize those things. And I rock ever so slightly in grandma's old rocking chair.

CR

Memories are made of . . .

ℛℛ

Good? - Or Bad?

William G. Mather, former President,
Cleveland Cliffs Iron Company

Are people basically good? Or are they basically bad?

That was a question that was asked of us while I was attending an Air Force Command and Staff College more years ago than I like to remember. Among our formal classes and lectures we would regularly meet in small groups of eight or ten members to view televised school presentations. As a part of the school curriculum we often carried on free and open group discussions. We might be evaluating what we had just seen or heard. Sometimes the discussions got quite passionate concerning the administration of the service or the nation or the actions of foreign nations and the motivation of the persons involved.

A class monitor was present and would frequently halt the discussion and call for a vote: "Are people basically good? Or bad?" No qualification or evasion or political verbosity would be permitted. Your vote must be up or down, one or the other. The majority vote moved both ways depending on the subject matter. One or two members seemed wedded to their religious imprint that all people are "good." The votes from the rest of us might depend on who we were discussing, someone like that North Korean "glorious leader" or Sadham Hussein or if we were talking about Mother Teresa.

Maybe we should be asking that question today right here at home? Read about some of our corporate executives currently on trial for pillaging their companies and stockholders and ask yourself that question.

Back during the economic collapse that occurred during the 1920s the Cleveland Cliffs Iron Company was in very bad financial straits. William G. Mather was the Company President. He knew his company's situation and that trouble was ahead. He didn't grab what money was left and run, as some of today's executives seem to have done. President Mather was concerned for the long-term survival of CCI – of "his" corporation – and for the welfare of the many employees who depended upon it for their livelihood. Operating capital was needed badly. Arranging a loan was critical to survival. Money was tight. To obtain the necessary financing lenders demanded more collateral. Not only were the assets of the company put up as collateral but also President Mather placed his personal fortune, his home and assets alongside those of the company to secure the loan. He then led the company through those hard times and on to the proud and prosperous company we see today.

William G. Mather had exhibited this strong moral character before, back about 1900 or so. At a collective meeting of the industrial giants of that time, he put forth an idea that almost alienated him with his fellow industrialists. Workers in that day were viewed as little more than tools to be used. They were bought as cheap as possible, kept only as long as they were needed, then discarded. If needs changed or a worker was injured they were terminated. End of story! There was no unemployment benefit or hospitalization or Medicaid. President Mather in a speech that would come to be known as the Magna Carta of labor stated his belief that a company had a responsibility to its workers. He said it wasn't right to fire a worker when business was down yet expect them to be there to be rehired again when they were needed. He concluded his speech with this statement put forth in the accepted social vernacular of that day:

"I would not like to close, however, without bearing witness to the feeling that upon us who have been more favored by education and opportunity, there rests that obligation so well expressed by the words 'noblesse oblige'."

That sounds like he might have been a democrat,

doesn't it? For the benefit of those among us unfamiliar with French, "noblesse oblige," freely translated, means that those of high birth, wealth, or social position must behave generously or nobly toward others – literally, "nobility obligates." They don't seem to be making many Company Presidents like that any more.

Another book churchgoers among us should be familiar with states President Mather's belief in another way: "To whom much is given, much is required." Many headlines in our newspapers seem to be telling us this is no longer true. So the question remains: are people basically good? Or basically bad? What do you think?

Weakness or Strength?

"Never apologize! It's a sign of weakness!" That's a remark in one of those shoot-em-up western movies made by a "macho" character played by John Wayne. A whole lot of us in the audience back then accepted that as gospel. "Yeah!" "Right on Big John!"

"The only thing worse than being vulnerable – is not being vulnerable." This comment was from a very close and wise lady friend of mine. To keep peace in my happy home I must assure my wife, Dorothy, that this was a friend of many years gone by. The passing of those years however has not diminished the truth of that observation.

To those of you who may be asking, "Who was John Wayne?" forget it. Stop reading and turn to the comic pages. For those of you who are still with me, keep those two statements in mind as we move on.

Human self-image – I think the psychiatrists call it the "ego" or the "id" or some term I can't even spell – is that part deep down inside of you that tells you who and what you think you are. It can be a very fragile thing in many of us and we protect it fiercely. A moment's reflection and we can probably all recall being "chopped off at the ankles," by a cutting remark or figuratively held at arm's length when we tried to reach out to someone.

You yourself, depending on your own level of self-confidence, may feel you have been attacked, diminished or put down by that sort of treatment. So where do we go from here? It depends on whether you subscribe to John Wayne's character or the philosophy of my friend.

Let me throw in a few bits and pieces of another quotation from a fella named Leo C. Reston: "In some small way, however small and secret, each of us is a little mad. . . . Everyone is lonely at bottom and cries out to be understood; but we can never entirely understand (anyone) else. . . . It is the weak who are cruel; gentleness is to be expected only from the strong. . . . You can understand people better if you look at them – no matter how old or impressive they may be – as if they are children. . . . most of us never mature; we simply grow taller. . . . The purpose of life is to matter – to count, to stand for something, to have it make some difference that we lived at all."

Next time you're walking into Wal-Mart or shopping in the mall and you notice someone approaching you with a scrunched up scowl on his or her face, really looking unhappy, here's a suggestion. Look straight at them so that when they look at you after you speak they'll know you're talking to them. Have a genuine smile on your face, nod your head or wave a hand a little as you offer a cheery "Good morning" or "It sure is a nice day, isn't it?" or whatever other positive happy statement occurs to you.

If the person continues to scowl and looks at you as

if they believe you're slipping your clutch, well, that's when you have to be strong enough emotionally to realize the problem is theirs and not yours. Most people will smile and respond with an equally cheerful comment. The beauty of the change in their expression is well worth the chance you took – the chance of being figuratively "cut off at the ankles." Remember, "gentleness" – "only from the strong." Roll the dice! Spread a little sunshine! You lose nothing you don't allow yourself to lose and you stand to gain having brought a little sunshine to the life of a stranger. You have "stood for something," you've "made some difference."

On the other hand you can play it safe. Shield yourself; protect your ego, your "id". Don't give anyone the chance to "put you down," to "chop you off at the ankles." We're back to the statements that began this article. Actually, it's never apologizing that's a sign of weakness – and what progress has ever been made unless someone was willing to take a chance, to be vulnerable? Is your individual cup of life "half full" or "half empty"? It's both. It all depends on how you look at that cup – and at the folks around you – that will determine the amount of sun shine in your own world.

CR

The only thing worse than being vulnerable
Is not being vulnerable.
(An old and dear friend told me this.)

CR

Somewhere the Sun is Shining

"Wars and rumors of wars." Boy! The news seems to be bad no matter where you stop, look or listen. Why is that? It's frustrating. I guess we've all experienced anger at one time or another. Maybe it's because of something the government does - or doesn't do? Maybe it's over some slight, real or imagined with a local business, or maybe with a neighbor who insists on firing up his snow blower at 6:00 AM to clear his driveway. As Bill Gates once said, "The world's not fair. Get used to it." Even with all these irritations I don't recall ever considering driving my car into my neighbor's garage and blowing myself up. For that there's gotta be a pretty serious hate – or a pretty unbalanced person – or both.

Every now and then someone suggests that children are becoming calloused to violence and contemptible of the law because of programs they see on television. How many of us in our younger years terrorized our parents by wrapping a sheet around our necks and leaping off the garage roof "like superman?" There was no television back then but we got the "man of steel" idea from comic books. We can argue about the extent of these influences but I don't think there's any question that our thinking is affected by everything we see, feel, hear, taste and smell and on and on. Sometimes it took a broken leg to show us we couldn't leap off the roof and fly through the air like superman. How much has really changed?

Entertainment however has exploded and seems to demand things more and more spectacular and mind boggling, the bloody and the gross. It all seems to be driven by a competition for a larger audience share. When the rest of us live with something long enough we become jaded. It becomes normal, acceptable causing the producers of this type of entertainment to reach still further.

If kids watch too much violence and disregarding of rules without some stabilizing counterbalancing influence they begin to accept it as the way things are and act accordingly. Now, what's the fundamental difference between kids and adults? It's size! That's it! We don't grow more mature we simply grow bigger. You may ponder this and say that adults are more aware that all that is make-believe. Maybe so but the appeal of this type of entertainment is to our pre-historic reptilian brain, that baser instinct that is said to be part of all of us. Remember that movie? "Dirty Harry"? – "Go ahead! Make my day!" Let's leave the movies and go a step further. I wonder if what we refer to as "the news" isn't constructed as "entertainment" also - produced to cater to those same base instincts. Blood! Gore! Sensationalism!

If a Girl Scout troop sets a new cookie sales record, it may (or may not) be mentioned in the newspapers in a small paragraph buried on page 8C somewhere. It's probably not mentioned at all on television. But if some guy shoots his wife it's on page one in ten point type – and leads television's six o'clock news – and again at seven – and eleven – and tomorrow morning and on and on.

When Hurricane Katrina hit Louisiana and the Gulf Coast how many times every day did we see the same pictures of those same folks stranded on that bridge - or that hungry, ragged, tearful mother and baby pleading for help? Every TV station in the nation and many overseas seemed to have that identical filmstrip which they ran over and over each day for almost a week. Photos were on the front page of every newspaper everywhere. How depressing can it get? Maybe it's an overload of reports of that sort that drive people to get in a car or an airplane and blow themselves up. If they also have the idea that "god" wants – well, that's a whole 'nother thing and we'd better not go there.

So what's the answer? What can you do about it? Let me make a suggestion. Turn the television off! It's that little button right there on the front – or maybe the side. Maybe you could talk to your husband or wife instead – if you still remember who and where they are. We shouldn't overdo anything. Too much sugar is not good for you so don't eat too much sugar. The same advice applies to McDonald's hamburgers and the evening news. I don't recommend burying your head in the sand but limit your intake. Remember to look up now and then and see the sunshine. There are many folks doing good things, enjoying life and trying to make life and living better for all people everywhere.

If you get hooked on too much of that depressing stuff you begin to think you've got all the cynical answers. That's when you're in trouble. Somebody once told me that you're not learning anything until you realize how much you don't know.

I was raised on a farm. I learned early on that life is a lot like a pasture. There's beauty and grass and flowers and that there are "cow-paddies" here and there too. As you walk along you may step in a "paddie." The trick is to wipe your foot and keep going, don't stay there and play in it. If you stay there, well, that's telling you something about you if you think about it.

CR

"If"

If you can keep your head when all about you
Are losing theirs and blaming it on you,
If you can trust yourself when others doubt you,
But make allowance for their doubting, too;
If you can wait and not be tired by waiting,
Or being lied about, don't deal in lies,
Or being hated, don't give way to hating,
And yet don't look too good nor talk too wise;
If you can dream and not make dreams your master,
If you can think, and not make thoughts your aim,
If you can meet with triumph and disaster,
And treat those two impostors just the same;
If you can bear to hear the truth you've spoken
Twisted by knaves to make a trap for fools,
Or watch the things you gave your life to, broken,
And stoop and build them up with worn out tools;
If you can make one heap of all your winnings,
And risk it on one turn of pitch-and-toss,
And lose, and start again at your beginnings,
And never breathe a word about your loss;
If you can force your heart and nerve and sinew
To serve your turn long after they are gone,

And so hold on when there is nothing in you
Except the will that says to them: "Hold on!"
If you can walk with crowds and keep your virtue,
Or walk with kings – nor lose the common touch,
If neither foes nor loving friends can hurt you,
If all men count with you, but none too much;
If you can fill the unforgiving minute
With sixty seconds worth of distance run,
Yours is the Earth and everything that's in it!
And what is more you'll be a man my son.

Rudyard Kipling

CR

Thoughts Along The Way

Thoughts Along The Way

Additional copies of this or any other of the author's books may be purchased through:

Still Waters Publishing
257 Lakewood Lane
Marquette, MI 49855-9508

(906) 249 9831

www.benmukkala.com
bmukk@chartermi.net

at the following prices:

"Thoughts Along the Way"	$ 15.95
"Life is Not a Destination"	$ 14.95
"Touring Guide; Big Bay & Huron Mountains	$ 9.95
"Come On Along"	$14.95
"Copper, Timber, Iron and Heart"	$15.95
Please add for shipping and handling	$ 5.00

Enjoy!

Ben Mukkala

Thoughts Along The Way

Author

Ben Mukkala

is a native of Marquette, Michigan where he graduate from Gravaraet High School and Ball State University in Indiana. He enlisted in the U. S. Air Force during the Korean War, rose through the ranks, served a tour of duty in Southeast Asia flying F-4 "Phantom" jet fighter-bombers in the Viet Nam conflict.

Ben retired in 1970 with the rank of Major. After retirement he flew various civilian aircraft, privately and commercially, sailed boats, and traveled.

He enjoys the outdoors and leads an active life. He began writing during his Air Force career and has been published in several flying and outdoor magazines and various newspapers. He has published several books.

He is the father of three daughters and one son, and stepfather to two sons and four daughters. He currently lives with his wife, Dorothy, on the shore of Lake Superior in Marquette, Michigan.

"Only a Life lived for others is a Life Worthwhile."

Albert Einstein